WINGED CRYPTIDS

HUMANOIDS, MONSTERS & ANOMALOUS CREATURES CASEBOOK

LON STRICKLER

BEYOND THE FRAY

Publishing

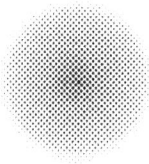

BEYOND THE FRAY

Publishing

Dedicated to the memory of my friend and colleague Jc Johnson, and to those who seek the truth.

ACKNOWLEDGMENTS

I want to thank the following friends and colleagues for their contributing research, investigations and assistance. They include, and are not limited to:

The members of Phantoms & Monsters Fortean Research, which includes Butch Witkowski, Sean Forker, Timothy Renner, Tobias & Emily Wayland, Manuel Navarette, Vance A. Nesbitt, Troy Noll, Jack Cary, Danielle Auclair, Rob Shaw, Brett Butler, Marcus Ellis, Ryan Fusco, Amy Bue & Luis Castillo.

I also wish to thank Stan Gordon, Jamie Brian, Albert S. Rosales, Ken Gerhard, Jonathan David Whitcomb, Ken Pfeifer, as well as all the eyewitnesses and the 'Phantoms & Monsters' readers. Special thanks to Donie Odulio for his wonderful illustrations.

Please be aware that a few of the eyewitness accounts in this book are written by ordinary people. Some text has been changed; but in some instances, it's been left unedited and as received. Thanks for your understanding.

Lon Strickler
www.phantomsandmonsters.com

Artwork Credit: Donie Odulio

INTRODUCTION

"Our world is more than what we can see, more
than what we have discovered and more
than what we can imagine."

– A CRYPTID INVESTIGATOR

———

What is a cryptid? **The Merriam-Webster dictionary defines a cryptid as 'an animal (such as Sasquatch or the Mothman) that has been claimed to exist but never proven to exist.'** I suppose that's a fair definition. But what evidence is needed for proof? Scientists and many researchers believe that a body, dead or alive, will be the only way to prove a cryptid's existence. Once again, I understand the logic behind this demand. But in the real world of cryptid investigation we rarely receive any clear-cut or precise physical evidence. We are compelled to rely on anecdotal testimony, eyewitness documentation and the occasional photograph or video.

I've researched and investigated a plethora of cryptid beings accounts, ever since my first personal encounter in 1981. Up until that experience I would occasionally probe a ghost or haunting case, usually within a day's drive from home. But my own brush with a cryptid creature suddenly changed my perspective on the unexplained, and I wanted to become a part of this genre of the paranormal.

Now, I earlier stated this was **'my first personal encounter.'** I was subsequently a part of another unexplained event in the Autumn of 1988. On this occasion, I was in the company of two other witnesses; an incident that began my intrigue with flying cryptids.

I was attending a Boy Scouts of America exhibition near Baltimore and bumped into an old friend who was there representing a troop from Adams County, Pennsylvania. Both of us had been Boy Scouts together and I was pleased to see that he had continued as a troop leader. We decided to grab a bite to eat and catch up a bit; it had been twelve years since we had seen each other. After a while the subject of my paranormal investigations entered the conversation. He had always been fascinated with ghost sightings at Gettysburg and the surrounding area and had camped near the battlefield on several occasions.

He proceeded to tell me that a few of the local troops had recently been camping at the old Camp Conewago and that some of the boys had reported hearing 'crying' sounds. They had been spooked so bad that a few had left their campsites early. He said that he and another scout leader were going to check out the area the following weekend and asked if I'd at least go up for the day and investigate with them. I accepted the invitation.

Camp Conewago is located north of New Oxford, Pennsylvania along the main Conewago Creek. It was established in 1919 for exclusive use by the local Boy Scouts of America. The area is rich in early colonial history since it was located on a major hunting route used by the Susquehannock Indians. Several attempts to establish settlements in this area failed because of Indian raids. As well, the Susquehannock constantly warred with neighboring tribes. They were eventually forced back into northeast Maryland and Delaware and the colonists were able to expand westward into the Allegheny Mountains. The area became an important trading stop for settlers to stock up on supplies and to get updates before heading into the wilderness.

I met my friend and his companion the following Friday at the campground. I was shocked at how little the place had changed. A flood of boyhood memories came over me while I walked around the cabins and the administration building. They wanted to know how long I planned to stay and said that they were going to setup camp in the same area of the reports. I told him I would stay for the weekend, so I grabbed my gear and followed them into the woods. I suppose we hiked about 500 yards or so before we came to the bank of the creek, then we followed the creek for another 300 yards until we reached an area near the fork. We setup 3 tents and had a nice fire going in short order. It was around 7:00 pm by this time, so we decided stay in camp for the remainder of the evening.

The first night was uneventful, though I sensed that something was watching us. I didn't say anything but kept my eyes open and head clear. These woods are somewhat thick with heavy ground cover and inhabited by a wide mix of wildlife.

The next morning was sunny and cool; a perfect day to explore the woods. We sat down to breakfast when my friend asked if we had heard footsteps and movement during the night. I said I had heard some movement but assumed it was either one of them. Nothing seemed to be disturbed in the campsite, so we dismissed it. I still had this lingering sense that we were being watched.

We spent the day walking for several miles through the woods and examining points of interest. I was thinking that this was going to be a quiet weekend. At about 6:00 pm we returned to our campsite and sat down to talk about any little thing that came into our heads.

Later that evening, at approximately 11:00 pm, we were sitting around the fire engaged in a conversation about football when suddenly a scream rang out downstream from our location. I thought it sounded like an owl at first. A few minutes later it happened again, and it distinctively sounded like a child's scream. I couldn't tell how far away it was, but it lasted for several seconds and seemed to fade in and out. We got up and walked a few yards into the woods expecting to hear the sound again. It was quiet for about an hour while we discussed what could have naturally caused that sound. I have heard bobcats, owls and rabbits scream and none sounded close to this. We agreed that it was comparable to the cries of a child.

We decided to stay up for the entire night. It was a bright moon that night and much of the woods and creek were visible. At approximately 1:00 am, I was walking the perimeter of our camp when I suddenly felt like something was again watching me. I returned to fire and mentioned that I felt uneasy.

We agreed to walk along the trail that paralleled the creek. We had only walked about 50 feet when, without warning, we recognized to our right a large dark figure with bright red eyes standing in the creek.

By the time we got our flashlights pointed in the being's direction, it suddenly jettisoned straight up into the air with an audible 'whoosh.'

A few seconds later we heard a loud scream, fading away as if it was moving away from us.

We hurried back to the campsite and compared our thoughts about this phantom we had just witnessed. My friend was visibly shaken and didn't talk for several minutes, until I prodded him for his recollection. The other companion was surprising calm and estimated that it was 6 foot or so in height, dark in color and seemed to have something extending from its back. I also noticed the structures on the back and commented that it reminded me of wings, but I was unsure.

We all agreed that it had bright red eyes.

My friend decided that he wanted to spend the remainder of the night in the administration building. Both he and the other guy walked back, but I decided to stay in the campsite for the remainder of the night. I really wanted to see this anomaly again; but nothing significant occurred during the night.

After the investigation and further research, I concluded that this creature or phantom was more than a simple spirit or energy. I was keenly aware of the sightings of the so-called 'Mothman' in West Virginia and it seemed that this being was somewhat similar in description. I have investigated this area since our sighting and have come up with very little evidence, though a report of a dark creature was made by a local resident a few years later.

In 2008, I received an email from a man who lived a mile or so upstream from this incident (near Dick's Dam). He stated that he had heard similar screams for many years and that the frightful sounds continue to this day.

A scout leader also emailed a few month later, he wanted to tell me that a few of the boys in his troop had witnessed what they described as a 'dragon' that was 6-foot-tall, with wings and a tail and looked like it had fur or feathers. He said that the boys seemed serious, but he thought they were 'showing off' and dismissed their claims; until later when he read the account of my 1988 experience.

Since that time, I have continued to check up on the area to see if anything strange develops. There have been five subsequent sightings of a similar winged humanoid along the Conewago Creek, downstream from my encounter. The last reported sighting was in 2015. The locals have dubbed the creature **Ole' Red Eyes.**

This casebook will present a wide variety of winged cryptid eyewitness reports that I have personally received and directly researched /investigated over the past three decades. I will also update the investigations conducted by Phantoms & Monsters Fortean Research that pertain to the Chicago area winged humanoid phenomena and other winged cryptid entities.

Lon Strickler

CHICAGOLAND SIGHTINGS CONTINUE

When I wrote '*Mothman Dynasty: Chicago's Winged Humanoids*' the last eyewitness report that I had included in the book involved a couple's encounter with large bat-winged humanoid in the Piotrowski Park parking lot in Chicago's Little Village community. This incident occurred on the evening of October 27, 2017. By that time, the sighting reports had begun to wane. I believed that the reason was related to the colder temperatures of the Autumn season. But as time went on sightings of a similar winged humanoid continued to trickle in. In fact, the incident locations were spreading beyond the Chicago suburbs and into other areas of Illinois, southern Wisconsin and most of Indiana.

As a result of a guest appearance on '*Beyond the Darkness*' with Dave Schrader, I received a telephone call from a witness who listened to the show.

AUGUST 27, 2017 – FOREST PARK, IL

THE WITNESS CALLED me on the morning of December 7, 2017. He stated that he was a retired police officer (25-year veteran) and resides in Kalamazoo, Michigan. He was visiting his mother on Sunday, August 27, 2017 (her birthday) at her residence in the Forest Park suburb of Chicago, IL.

At approximately 8:45 pm local time, he volunteered to walk his mother's dog before he left to drive home to Michigan. His mother's caregiver (a neighbor) usually did this task.

As he walked west on Jackson Blvd, in front of the Howard Mohr Community Center, he noticed something crouched on the roof, behind the facade of the building next door (west) to the community center. Since it was dusk and that there was a bit of light coming from a streetlight, the witness was able to observe whatever this was.

He had stopped walking and was fifty or so feet away from, what he described as, a 'dark gargoyle' that was looking directly at him. The dog, a Standard Poodle, was restless and began to bark. The being stood up and made a growling-like sound, very guttural and menacing. The witness noticed that the eyes were small but had a distinct reddish glow. The being had a body shape that was resembled a human man but was gaunt and dark gray in color. There were large wings folded outward from its back. These were very similar to the typical image of a gargoyle, but much larger. The height was around six feet or so. The head was somewhat conical and small compared to the rest of the body. It had long arms with claw-like hands, that swayed back and forth in front of the being.

After watching for about ten to fifteen seconds (he also had to maintain control of the dog, which was barking and pulling on the lead), the wings 'snapped' from the back of the being and spread out to a full span. The wings were very distinct with a dark membrane covering. He estimated the span was about fifteen feet and extended high above the being.

Then the being's wings dropped to its side and it quickly propelled itself into the air, heading south in the direction of the Metro station. It made no sound as it ascended.

The witness quickly returned to his mother's house, but he did not want to upset her by mentioning his encounter. He told me that he had not heard of the sightings in Chicago and that he questioned what he had seen, until he heard the radio show. This is the first time he has talked about the incident.

The witness was very convincing and seemed relieved that he was able to safely recount his encounter. I believe that he may have been a member of the local police (Forest Park or Chicago) at some point in his career; but he never acknowledged it. He asked me not to use his name. Not even his initials.

JANUARY 28, 2018 – WILMINGTON, IL

I RECEIVED the following email on Sunday January 28, 2018 at 6:50 am:

> "I live in Wilmington, IL, about 15 mins south of Joliet. I frequent my outside steps in between 1-4 am pretty much nightly for a smoke or two, and I'm constantly observing the skies out of pure fascination. I only mention this because I have never, in the year and 1/2 of living in this home, experienced anything as incredible, yet terrifying, as this sighting!
>
> At exactly 4:36 am (Sunday January 28, 2018 local time) I was sitting on my step and I was looking up at the sky, when suddenly my eyes were immediately drawn to what appeared to be a weird hybrid mix of an owl and a bat. To me the size was approximately that of a large raccoon. I even would go as far as saying it was a bit larger. For some reason, I was frozen

solid with my eyes locked on this thing. I found it weird that even with how dark it was outside it seemed close enough for me to notice details of it to the point of realizing that it appeared brownish/greyish in color and the wings had a bat-like appearance.

I felt a little weird explaining to my husband that it was triangular and resembled the biggest moth ever. Instantly my head went to the Mothman! It was shockingly fast, and it never made a sound; nor did it flap its wings. It just glided west and disappeared as fast as it seemed to appear. This creature even looked to have passed through a very old tall tree in my yard, and even though it was hard to obviously tell whether it went above my tree or literally through the branches, I still never heard even a small rustle from the breeze it would've created due to its speed. I apologize for the novel I am clearly writing, but I want to give you as many details as possible as I also have a couple questions about details from other noted sightings of this.

The most interesting part of my experience is that I felt and still currently feel a sense of dread and impending doom. But at the same time, it felt like this creature perched itself onto my roof and was just glaring at me until I went inside. Whether this is true I don't know for sure, but I've never felt watched like that before. After it had essentially disappeared into the night and I was in disbelief I started to hear what sounded like a bat screech, but with a lower tone. It sounded much larger than a bat. It happened twice within about 5 seconds apart from each screech and I then booked it inside to explain it all to my husband. It is currently 1 hour since the sighting and I still feel as if I'm being preyed upon. I am very curious to know if others who have contacted you have had similar dreadful feelings and heard these screeches?

Please get back to me at your earliest convenience and thank you so much for taking the time to read this! CH"

By chance, I was awake when the email reached me. I immediately contacted the witness by email and then left a note for the Chicago Phantom Task Force. I received a telephone number and called the witness. The description of the winged being was that it had a triangular shape; reminiscent of the 2011 photo from 8/22/2011 at 63rd and Pulaski Rd in Chicago, IL. The witness said that the being was flying at an altitude of approximately fifty feet and anywhere from four to five feet in length. The wingspan was approximately five feet on either side of the body, which was thin and dark in color. She also noticed a sheen on the body; like it may have had reptilian-like skin and wet. The wings were membraned but shaped like that of a huge owl. She was amazed at how quickly it glided and that it did not flap its wings or make a sound.

Shortly after the sighting, the witness heard screeches that sounded like children. She was sure this being was watching her and that she reacted like something sinister was about to occur. She went indoors and told her husband. She then found the descriptions of the Chicago sightings and contacted me.

It must also be noted that the witness and others in her neighborhood have experienced UFO sightings and flashes of light since December 2017. The location is just east of the Kankakee River surrounded by several nature preserves; situated between power generating stations and a chemical plant. There is a lot of wetland throughout the area. As well, the weather had been unseasonably warm, possibly prompting the reappearance of these winged beings.

JANUARY 27, 2018 – LEXINGTON, IL

I WAS CONTACTED by a witness on January 30, 2018 in reference to an unknown flying being in Lexington, Illinois. The information is comparable to that of the Wilmington, IL witness, including other bizarre activity:

"My wife and I moved to Lexington, Illinois in April 2016. During that first summer here, we heard a lot of stories, from residents that we talked to.

Back on January 27, 2018, I wasn't sleeping well because the local coyote pack was getting riled up about something. They were extremely vocal that night. I'm usually a deep sleeper but they woke me up with their incessant yipping, barking and howling. It sounded like a hunt was on.

I got up and decided to use the bathroom, after I did a quick check outside from our windows. While in there I heard what could be liked to an animal-like screech, like the Rous from the 'Princess Bride' film and a deep bass "whoo." I thought it was odd. So, I looked out our bathroom window and saw a large shadow pass under a streetlight about 30 feet from our place. It did it a couple times before a creature, like the witness from Wilmington, IL described, landed. It made no sound when it flared its wings as it landed in a tree not more than ten feet from our place. A local creek is about sixty to seventy feet away from our place and about the same distance from the tree this being was perched in. It walked with a kind of hop. The feet had a splayed three-clawed foot, with digits like a sloth. I did not get a good look at the torso or how its arms and grasping digits looked, but the way it landed it looked like it had paws, but I'm not sure. I never got a good look at the head.

I observed it for a few minutes before it made that unnerving screech-hoot sound about four times before it just glided out of the tree towards the creek, in a south-southwest direction of the Mackinaw River. The coyotes started up again with their noise, but I like they were following.

I don't think it knew it was being observed. It was more unnerving than the times a Bigfoot made visits to my family's property when I was young, or the night when something literally destroyed two of our mares. I remember enough of that night that I have nightmares. But not this thing. It just unnerved me. But one thing I did notice was the stench of blood in the air. I don't know if you've been hunting, but that blood smell when you are field dressing a deer or antelope, that was the smell it left behind. This occurred between 2:30 am and 2:45 am on 1-27-18.

The Wilmington, IL witness reported helicopter activity. In this area it ramps up in the late fall early winter, between 11 pm and 1:45 am. It quits and starts up again at around 2:30-2:45 am until around 4 am.

One night I was out for a quick walk and heard an odd chopper sound. It sounded like a Blackhawk but weird, like it had baffling on. But the chop of the blades is unmistakable. That night there was a clear enough sky for a full moon. I saw the silhouette, but the tail section was shaped like the rear tail of a Comanche helicopter. It flew over the cornfields and little forest area nearby and the Mackinaw River for hours, back and forth.

One night in November 2016, I got curious enough to try out my night vision camera. I waited for the chopper to come, right like clockwork it began a 5x5 search pattern. Through the lens I observed two domes under the fuselage, by the cockpit. To my eye not glued to my eyepiece, one was emitting a rather powerful search light, but it was concentrated on the river area. It banked north and came close by our place. I saw a brightness emitting from the other dome. I couldn't see it with my naked eye, but it was there on screen. It overloaded *the optics on my camera. Also, the video that I recorded on the flash drive was corrupted and not retrievable. The battery supply burst and the main board was toast.*

That same night I was woken by the sound of diesel engines, but not semi diesel. I looked out on PJ Keller Highway, and there was a small convoy of three MRAPS, four Hummers, and five MATVS. A couple Hummers had that new .50 caliber mini gun mounted. The rest had either the M2 or M240 mounted. They all looked like they were primer grey colored. They stopped at intervals on either side of the small bridge fifty feet away. Troops dismounted from the MRAP and MATV. They had rifles and strange body armor. They kept the vehicle lights on. I took out my field spotter glasses and got a better look; fast entry helmets, balaclavas, four eye night vision sets. Dull finished metallic looking body armor on the vest, arms, legs and neck. They all carried combat sabers, and either FN2000 rifles or rifles that looked like the XM25, 26, 27 prototypes.

A team of three went into the woods off to the right of the road. If you are headed west, by the cemetery. They were gone about ten minutes, when a couple shots rang out and all the troops came out of the woods in a hurry, entered the vehicles and took off.

The helicopter flyovers stopped until this past August. It's like clockwork. Monday, Wednesday, Friday, Saturday and Sunday. 11 pm to 12:45 am, then 2:30 am to 4:00 am. One is currently flying over as I type this on 1-31-2018 at 12:30 am.

I prefer to remain anonymous for now. I worked as a civilian independent contractor in the Dakotas for about 8 years. I was an advisor in the Golden Coyote exercises in the Black Hills of South Dakota, and the bombing range recovery in the Badlands of South Dakota. I grew up in a military family, in all branches. I've been around military vehicles since I could remember. I couldn't join because of a health problem they detected."

I don't know how much the military activity was related to the winged being's presence, but the information was quite interesting.

FEBRUARY 2, 2018 – CHICAGO, IL

THE FOLLOWING report was received and investigated by Manuel Navarette at UFO Clearinghouse:

"I was walking toward my apartment with my best friend and another girlfriend after getting off the Green Line train. It was about 11 pm on Friday, February 2, 2018. We were right next to the parking lot beside to the YMCA when we saw something land across the street from us. The streetlight gave it some illumination along with the moonlight and it looked like a tall man, but it had a very large black pair of wings. Now I know we had been drinking a bit, but I was sober enough to know reality from hallucination. Besides, seeing this thing was enough to scare anyone sober in a heartbeat. Seeing a man with wings was already freaky enough, but when we saw what could only be described as its eyes, it sent a chill down my body. The eyes were bright red and seemed to glow from within. It looked at us for maybe five seconds before it spread its wings as wide as they could apparently go, started to flap and it then slowly gained altitude. It flapped those wings faster and faster until it was above the building and gone. We could not get back to my apartment fast enough. Once inside we closed and bolted the door shut."

Manuel provided a later update:

"I spoke with two of the witnesses yesterday and both seem to be sincere and well-educated professionals. Both individuals, a male, twenty-six years old and a female, twenty-eight years old, had been at their jobs for five and seven years respectively and both do admit to drinking. Both witnesses confirm that they have never done anything stronger than marijuana.

The third witness was unable to meet with us. He indicated that he would get in touch with me on a later date. I was given some background information on the third witness. He is around the same age as both the witnesses I interviewed, professional and educated as well.

According to the witnesses, they had gone out after work and had arrived at the Green Line Station at Harlem and Lake at about 11:30 pm. They headed to the male witnesses' apartment which was about three blocks from the train station.

As they were walking toward the apartment, they reportedly saw a large human-shaped entity with large black wings landing across the street from them. They described the entity as being approximately six to six and a half feet tall, very skinny and lanky with very large wings which were approximately ten foot wide.

When asked how they determined the wing's width, they said that the entity had spread its wings to their full width before taking off into the air. They both described the entity's eyes as bright ruby red which glowed from within as it stared at them for a few seconds before ascending. They state that the entity vigorously flapped its wings as it climbed, rising above the buildings, then out of sight.

The witnesses stood there for about a minute before heading toward their apartment. They described their mood as stunned and shocked. They both said that they never felt scared or fearful of their sighting.

Both witnesses were interviewed individually and then together. Both corroborated each other stories with no deviation. When asked questions meant to embellish or deviate from their stories, both witnesses quickly corrected the investigator indicating that there was no deception in the accounts. It is the investigator's opinion that both witnesses are credible and that the story seems to be truthful."

This is an area where there have been other sightings and encounters (at least three reports within a one-mile radius previously given to us). The vigorous flapping of the wings before ascension is a bit of a variation, though there is no detail as to the wing structure. There were a few more unseasonably warm days in the Chicago, which may account for a continuation of the sightings.

SEPTEMBER 2016 NEAR WHITEWATER, WI

ON FEBRUARY 19, 2018 I received a telephone call from a witness in southeast Wisconsin.

In late September 2016 at approximately 10 pm the witness was driving east on E. State Rd. 59 (S. Janesville St.) approximately seven miles west of Whitewater, Wisconsin. She was heading home after visiting her daughter.

Suddenly a 'man-like' being with huge bat-like wings glided in front of her and behind another car, flying from right to left at an altitude of ten feet or so above the road. The witness was totally shocked at what she was seeing. The being's body was human-like in shape; about six feet in length and the wingspan was at least twice the body length. The wings were membraned like that of a bat and never moved or flapped. The entire being was dark in color. There seemed to be a structure along the top of its head, but no eyes or facial features were seen.

The witness' reaction was to hit the gas pedal and to get out of the area. The driver in front of her must have noticed the winged being as it emerged from the right and sped away as well.

There were other sighting reports from southern Wisconsin and northern Illinois that the task force was investigating at the time. The witness had told very few people about her encounter but decided, with her husband's encouragement, to come forward and call me. Her demeanor was a bit anxious, though she seemed relieved to unburden herself.

SUMMER 2013 – DES PLAINES, IL

VERY SOON AFTER I received the Whitewater, Wisconsin report, an account that occurred in Des Plaines, Illinois was forwarded to me:

> "On a summer evening in 2013 my son and I were leaving my friend's house, who lived near Des Plaines, Illinois. Her driveway is about a quarter mile long. There are no lights along the driveway. About halfway to the road, my son yelled out 'what's that?' I was startled and slammed on my brakes. 'What are you yelling for?' 'There, in the tree!' I answered, 'What are you looking at?'
>
> I glanced up into the tree, and noticed talons wrapped around the large lower branch. The tree was thick with foliage, so it was hard to make out what it was. I figured it was just an owl or eagle, but as we watched the tree began to move, like

there was something very heavy in the tree. The headlights were pointed directly at the tree, so there was some light.

Then suddenly, a human-like figure dropped from the tree and landed upright on the ground in front of us. It was dark grey in color. As I looked at the clawed feet and muscular legs, I noticed the bottom tip of folded wings behind it. My eyes followed up the human-like body, which looked like dark grey skin. The head and face literally reminded me of a gargoyle; snarling features and evil looking. The eyes were large and reflected an orange color. I believe it also had short horns on the side of the head. 'OMG, what is that?' At the same time my son begged me 'Let's go! Let's go!' The beast opened its huge wings and literally took off and up over the car!

I called my friend on my cellphone as we were driving home. I told her what we witnessed. She was totally dumbfounded. She told me that she had never seen anything like that. While driving, I ask my son what he thought he saw. He called it a 'Batman.' I simply responded 'OK.' But I thought gargoyle or some other mythical creature. I was deeply affected by this beast and have carried this odd feeling that it would remember us.

I've been reading about the sightings in Chicago and wonder if there is a connection. I fear that a terrible event may occur in the city. My son is in college in Chicago, and I work downtown. I am scared for us. I swear what I have described is true. I wish to remain anonymous and I don't seek any recognition."

I contacted the witness by email. Her email address was from a Chicago law firm and since her name is part of the firm name, I can assume she is a partner.

FEBRUARY 15, 2018 – ZION, IL

THE FOLLOWING account was recently received by Manuel Navarette at UFO Clearinghouse on March 2, 2018:

> *"I was driving home on I-94. I pulled into the TA truck stop to get something to eat before finishing my trip home. It was about 11:30 pm (February 15, 2018) when I left the store and got in my car. As I was pulling out of the parking lot to get onto the interstate, I noticed what looked like a large person standing on the opposite side of the road. This thing looks right at me with very bright red eyes and then opened a huge pair of wings and started to fly off. It reminded me of a huge bat. The whole damn thing took less than five seconds. I know what I saw. It looked like a giant, skinny man with a large pair of wings and red eyes. I'm not sure what to tell you that it was, but I can assure you it's something I've never seen on the Discovery Channel before."*

Manuel offered an update:

> *"I spoke with the witness regarding his sighting. The witness is a 37-year-old male who lives in Gurnee, Illinois but works in Racine, Wisconsin. The witness works as an industrial welder and has worked at the same position for 21 years. The witness states that he takes the same route five to six times a week and has stopped at the truck stop multiple times.*
>
> *The witness states that he stopped at the TA truck stop and spent roughly ten minutes inside the store. The witness got in his car and started headed back toward the highway when he saw what looked like a large winged humanoid. He stated that the encounter did not last very long and that the being was solid black with a large pair of wings. The creature was*

hunched over and appeared to be looking at something on the ground. The witness says that when he illuminated the creature, it looked up and stood. Then the witness says that the creature took a couple of steps away from him and started flapping its wings and took off into the air.

The witness seemed very sincere, albeit scared and a little bewildered. He stated that the creature was out of sight within a matter of seconds. When asked if others might have seen it, the witness states that there must be others because it is a busy truck stop."

The location is in Zion, Illinois and appears to be approximately a 1/2 mile south of the Wisconsin/Illinois border. I believe Manuel posted flyers at the truck stop in order to gather witnesses.

JULY 15, 2006 – EAGLE, WI

ON MARCH 3, 2018, I received the following account:

"I would like to thank you for your site. I don't feel ridiculed telling my story to you. Even if I am, I don't care what the skeptics think. I know what I saw, and it is the truth.

On July 15, 2006, my husband and I were in the process of moving from Milwaukee, Wisconsin, to a small area between Whitewater and Eagle, WI. It was about 9:30 pm and there was a bright full moon in a clear sky.

We were traveling on Highway 59 East, past Eagle, and turned onto Road X, a somewhat desolate stretch of road. A thin band of trees are on each side of the road, with open fields behind them. This area is about 18 miles east of Whitewater, located between Eagle and North Prairie, WI.

My husband was driving. His two young children were in the back seat asleep. Suddenly, something swooped over the trees on our left and lowered down in front of the car windshield, then upwards again over the treetops to our right. It then glided at a slow ascent over the field. I would describe it as a man with bat-like features, flying like a bat.

This creature was as real as you and I are. We had a very good look at it. It was long, six to seven feet in length. I say length, because it was flying sideways, looking into the car, much like a swimmer doing the sidestroke. It was a dark grey, very leathery skin, one wing kind of tucked into its side (the one nearer the ground) and the other flapping while it flew. The wing was huge and looked exactly like bat. What got me the most were the eyes. They were very round. Where the whites would be, it looked rheumy. That's the best way to describe it. The irises were a very pale blue. I was not afraid, but I was astounded and excited. My husband was shaken and would not stop when I asked him to.

I hope this will also bring more people forward who have seen this mystery creature, or other creatures as well. I was reading recently online of a woman in Minong, WI, who in about 1960, also had seen a creature of this description. I notice that some who have witnessed this, compare it to the creature from the movie, 'Jeepers Creepers.' There were definite similarities. I had never seen the movie prior to my sighting. - DS"

This sighting was on the edge of the Kettle-Moraine Low Prairie State Natural Area. The pale blue eyes and the sideways flight using one wing is quite interesting. Out of all the sightings I have received over the years, these characteristics are unique. Another example of how bizarre and mysterious these beings really are.

APRIL 10, 2018 – CHICAGO, IL

I RECEIVED a telephone call from two eyewitnesses on the night of Tuesday, April 10, 2018.

The witness stated that on Tuesday, April 10, 2018, at 8:30 pm CT (local time) she and her partner were in the area of S. University Ave. & E. 72nd St. (Woodlawn community) picking up their daughter, when they both noticed a huge dark winged being gliding overhead. The being was at an approximate altitude of fifty feet or so, swiftly gliding north towards downtown Chicago. They watched the being until it was shielded by trees. The area was well-lit by the streetlights. It made no sound and never flapped its wings.

Both witnesses agreed and described the being as an 'owl man' with a wingspan of 'at least' fifteen feet and a thin human-like body of approximately six feet in length. They could not see a head but did notice appendages underneath. The wings were shaped like an owl, which the witnesses have seen in the neighborhood. They emphatically stated that this 'was not' an owl or any other bird. They were familiar with blue herons and sandhill cranes since they are both lifelong residents of the Chicago metro area, and that there was 'no chance' that this was one of those creatures.

I asked the witnesses if they thought if it could have been a flying device or drone. Both confidently stated that this was a living being and not mechanical.

As soon as they arrived home (which was less than a block from where they observed the being) they Googled 'human bird in Chicago' and my contact information was the result of the search. Both seemed nervous and confused by what they saw and asked what I knew about this winged being. Neither witness was aware of the previous sightings in the Chicago metro area since early 2017. They chose to remain completely anonymous.

APRIL 11, 2018 – CHICAGO, IL

I RECEIVED a text message on Wednesday, April 11, 2018, at 11:07 am ET:

> "Hi - I was on Reddit and came across a post with a link to your website about the thing that is flying around Chicago. I was driving down Lake St., and had just turned off Central Ave. It was between Austin Ave. and Lake St. - near the Chicago/Oak Park border last night shortly after 8:00 pm. I was heading west and just slightly to my north I saw this massive thing in the air. It swooped behind an apartment building so my view was blocked. I only saw it for maybe eight to ten seconds, but it was enough to leave me absolutely stunned. I grew up in Chicago and have NEVER seen anything like that before in the city. My first reaction was maybe it was something that escaped from a wildlife rescue but - this thing was massive - like easily over ten feet wide. Now that I know I'm not crazy and other people have seen it I feel better. Like for real, it was huge. I've never seen a bird that large before. I spent time in the Army and was Military Police - and this thing was no drone, that's for sure! I keep trying to come up with any logical explanation for what I saw last night, but I'm completely baffled. - KM"

I contacted KM by telephone the same evening and conducted an interview.

The witness states that she had just turned west onto Lake

St. from N. Central Ave. It was close to 8:00 pm CT (local time) because she was meeting a friend. As she proceeded west on Lake St. and approached N. Menard Ave., she noticed a huge flying being gliding above a nearby four story apartment building, approximately sixty feet above the ground. The flying being ducked behind the apartment building and she lost sight of it. The witness estimates that she watched the flying being for eight to ten seconds. She turned into an alleyway in order to get another look at the being but was unsuccessful.

The witness states that the being had a ten foot plus wingspan with bat-like wings and dark in color. The wings never flapped. The body was quite long and thin, approximately six to eight feet in length and there were two appendages / legs, since she noticed a separation. She did not notice any further structures on the body or head.

The witness did seem a bit nervous while talking to me and was very surprised at the number of sightings in the general area since early 2017. She had no previous knowledge of the phenomenon.

APRIL 12, 2018 – CHICAGO, IL

ON FRIDAY, April 20, 2018, I received a telephone call from a woman in Chicago, in reference to a sighting that her and a friend had on Thursday, April 12, 2018, at approximately 7:15 pm CT. It was early dusk, but still plenty of ambient light available.

The two elderly women were walking north along N. Greenway Ave. towards the intersection with W. Diversey Pkwy. in the West Lakeview neighborhood of Chicago.

They both heard a brief 'deep bellowing sound' emanating from the area of the intersection. As they both looked towards that direction, a dark winged being flew in front of them, towards the west, at an altitude of fifteen feet or so. Then suddenly the being 'vanished' from their sight, as if it had been 'swallowed up' somehow. There was no further sound or remnants of the being. The women told me that a man across the street also observed the incident, and immediately began to run in the opposite direction. The women stated that they were 'paralyzed' and could not move or talk for almost 20 seconds after the event. They then hurriedly walked towards their residence.

When they returned home, they were 'confused and drained of energy.'

They were fearful of what they saw and agreed not to report the sighting. A week after the incident, one of the women had noticed some of the previous internet reports of a similar winged being in the Chicago. At that time, she contacted me. I was eventually able to talk with both witnesses.

The observation of the winged being was very brief, but the women stated that it was almost black in color and that the wings were somewhat folded along the body, which was six to seven feet in length. No other details of the winged being were available.

The witnesses are very private people and insisted that they not be contacted by other investigators.

This is the first reported sighting that included details of possible inter-dimensional abilities of a flying winged humanoid. This location was a few blocks south of Wrigley Field. There had been an earlier report of a running humanoid that disappeared on the Magnificent Mile building roof.

APRIL 2017, NEAR MUKWONAGO, WI

On April 29, 2018, I received the following account. I quickly followed-up with a telephone interview:

"*In mid-April of last year (2017), I was sitting inside my car which was parked facing north in the driveway at my home, located between Eagle-Palmyra and Mukwonago, WI. I had been having an extended phone conversation with an old friend on the way home and had not gone inside the house yet and remember looking at the clock-radio at approximately 10:45 pm. It had been a dreary, overcast, misty and rainy day, one of those days where it just drizzled non-stop, but never turned into an outright heavy downpour.*

While shooting the breeze about the day's events, I looked up briefly from the dash of my vehicle (a minivan) and momentarily noticed 'someone' who was very, very tall, and very dark just standing in the rain, about five to ten feet (at most) in front of the vehicle, perfectly still with raindrops dripping down off their body. It was rather dark, but there is a post-lamp at the end of the driveway near the road, about forty to fifty feet from where I was parked, so I could make out the silhouette with a slight bit of backlighting from the lamp. As I had been in mid-conversation, I looked away for one-second, my brain not immediately registering or comprehending what I had just seen, so within about a second and a half, I did a 'double-take,' as I suddenly thought, 'Wait a minute. What the **** was THAT?!'

As I forcibly directed my unbelieving gaze back up toward the front of the vehicle, I said to my friend on the phone, 'You're not going to believe this...,' and I proceeded to quickly turn on my headlamps and stare at this 'thing' as I gave a concise, yet detailed-as-possible description to my buddy while I was literally shaking and scared out of my wits. I was looking at a creature, for lack of a better term, that essentially looked like a seven foot bat / reptile of some sort. The head was at the level of the roof of my minivan, or slightly more elevated than my roof, and it was standing perfectly still just staring right at me. Its eyes were large, taking up a significant portion of the thing's head, from what I could make out, and although they were dark, like large black eyeballs, there was a glint of reflection in them which allowed me to discern that they were, in fact, definitely its eyes. It was haunting, for lack of a better way to put it. I'm creeped out just recalling the memory of the event! I also noticed that besides the creature's height, it was also quite large, possessing extraordinarily swarthy coloration, though slightly reflective, like skin or scales of some kind, not feather nor fur-covered from what I could tell. It was at least as wide as a very large man, but did not seem 'stocky,' as it were, and as I stared at it uncomfortably. I realized that it had huge wings, but they were wrapped around its body, exactly as a bat wraps its wings around its body while sleeping upside-down. Except, this thing was standing right-side-up, looking right at me, or almost 'through me.' It seemed OMINOUS.

My initial reaction was to tell my buddy on the phone that I was looking right at a giant 'bat-dragon looking thing,' to which he asked if I had been drinking or something, and I assured him that this thing was really standing there, and I was looking right at it. The bottom of its face (mouth?) was completely covered by its fleshy-looking wings wrapped around its body, and I could tell that whatever it was, it was certainly physically powerful, as the rather wide 'shoulder-wing' area appeared to show some manner of musculature. The way it was standing there, it seemed to likely have a general humanoid body-shape under the wrapped wings. I could not see its 'feet' since it was standing too close to the vehicle, nor could I see anything below about what I imagine would be considered knee-level on the creature. That's how close it was. I was very afraid. As soon as I had given my friend on the phone a description of what I was seeing, I noticed that it seemed to very quickly 'move,' although I did not see it unwrap its wings, or walk, per se, but there was simply what I will describe as a brief blur in the headlights, and it was gone. The entire time of observation before it vanished was realistically only about twelve-seconds, but considering the uneasy, wayward way that thing was leering at me, even that was too long!

Now, being on the verge of panicking, my friend, who was still on the line, attempted to make light of the situation, and although appreciative of his friendly candor, I got out my trusty LED emergency flashlight from the glove box and told him that I was not about to continue sitting out there any longer, and was retiring to the house indoors for the night! The remainder of that evening was uncomfortable, but uneventful.

I mentioned the experience to one other friend, a work associate who has had a lifelong interest in such unusual subject matter. But I otherwise kept it to myself for fear of ridicule, and also because the experience, albeit brief, came across as more than just a sighting of a rare animal or cryptozoological remnant of some archaic species long thought extinct, but seemed to be something 'else.' Something of an entirely 'different nature.'

Even more unsettling was that about a week to two weeks later, that same old buddy I had been speaking with the night of the experience called me to inquire if I had watched or heard the news the previous evening. I informed him that I had not. After having initially assumed that I had gone completely out of my mind, for well over a week, he informed me that my sanity had been vindicated. Numerous encounters with the same creature had been recently reported in Chicago and northern Illinois, in largely populated areas.

To date, I have not had any further visits from the creature.
- MG"

I called the witness and asked him to detail the encounter once again. There was very little deviation from the written report, other than that the winged being had a dark grayish color and literally vanished without unfurling its wings. The conversation was very intense, and the witness was noticeably affected by the encounter, even thirteen months since the incident. The event was comparable to the Bolingbrook, Illinois encounter, which reminded me of the 'Vore' creatures in the 'Beastmaster' film. The witness shared his name and contact information with me. I forwarded the witness' information with Tobias and Emily Wayland who later investigated the location and interviewed MG.

APRIL 18, 2018 – MILWAUKEE, WI

I RECEIVED the following account by email on Monday, May 1, 2018

"*I discovered your website after doing some looking around on the web regarding flying creature reports. After reading through your blog I felt comfortable to report what happened to me and my boyfriend recently in Milwaukee, WI.*

This occurred on April 13, 2018, at about 10-10:30 PM. We were parked in the lot next to the (REDACTED).

My boyfriend looked up and totally freaked out when he says he saw a pair of large glowing red eyes staring right back at him. I looked up and saw something standing in front of my car with two glowing red eyes. It made a sound of chirping sound that we heard when we turned down the radio. When we moved, it put what looked like a hand on the hood of the car and then we saw what looked like wings spread wide open. I panicked and turned on the car which automatically turned on my headlights and it lit up what looked like a large bat. It had black skin that looked like glossy, wet leather that shined in the light. It then screamed at us, pushing its head out and its arms back and then flew up into the air. You could hear the wings flapping as it jumped up and within a few seconds, it landed behind my car. Its body was still able to be seen when I pressed the brakes and the brake lights shined.

Both of us were screaming at this point when it flew back up in the air and landed about six feet from the passenger side door where my boyfriend sat. We wasted no time in trying to get out of there. As we backed up and whipped the car around, we saw it land in front of us off to the side of the car about three feet away. I honked my horn and turned on my high beams and it screamed again and flew up into the air. We screeched onto (REDACTED) and headed toward I think it was (REDACTED) when my boyfriend says he saw it land again just off the road on his side of the car. We did not stop to investigate and floored the car to get out of there. We got onto (REDACTED) and were passing the apartment buildings when we saw something fly right over the car, lower than the lamp post, screaming as it flew out of sight.

We got to my house and stayed in the car for about 15-20 minutes, I was hysterical and crying and my boyfriend was shaken up. It took me another thirty minutes to get myself together and go drop off my boyfriend and drive myself back home. I have had repeated nightmares since then and it's been difficult to sleep without the closet light on. My boyfriend also says he has had nightmares.

I hope you believe me and that you don't think I'm crazy. It could not have been a large bird like some people seem to say it might be. I know whatever it was must have been intelligent, it's just a feeling that I have that tells me so.

Thank you, JR"

I contacted the witness and received the following information:

"I estimate it stood about seven feet tall, and the wingspan has to be about seven to eight feet or more wide. I almost got the feeling like it was toying with us. It knew we were scared shitless and it toyed with that by scaring us even further.

As far as physical reactions, it took me a few hours to finally get back to somewhat normal. I threw up twice just from jitters and I had a feeling like I was being watched, even though the curtains were closed.

Currently, I still feel like I'm being watched, almost like I'm marked in some way. Last night was the first night I slept without the lights being on and it took me about an hour and half to finally fall asleep. It's put me off to wanting to go out at night anymore, even though I need to get out in order to finish college by July.

We've been out to that same spot countless times previous and this is the first time we've seen this thing. JR"

One of the more horrifying encounters I've ever run across. The sightings in Wisconsin were beginning to increase. The witness shared her name and contact information. Tobias and Emily Wayland did investigate the encounter. I redacted the location information in order to prevent a group of Milwaukee-based investigators from disrupting the investigation and harassing the witnesses.

2

A LIFE ALTERING ENCOUNTER

SUMMER 1981 – CICERO, IL

On May 25, 2018, I was contacted by an eyewitness who, as a child of 13 years of age, had a remarkable encounter with a winged humanoid in Cicero, IL. The year was 1981 and the witness, who I will refer to as 'MR', experienced a life-changing event.

MR contacted me by email and asked to speak by telephone. I instantly had the sense that this interview would be significant, so I requested MR call me at his earliest convenience. We were talking within 10 minutes.

MR introduced himself and immediately started to tell me his account. He prefaced his story by saying that he had not known of the winged humanoid sightings reported throughout the Chicago metro area, until he stumbled upon an article two days previous. He was stunned by the revelations in the article; dozens of sightings that closely resembled his encounter in Cicero in 1981. But MR's narrative was different, because his encounter with the winged humanoid altered his overall beliefs and perspective of the world.

MR was a 13-year-old boy in 1981 who, through his own description, had suffered terrible abuse during his young life. On one evening, like many previous evenings, he sought solitude in his backyard. For whatever reason, he was able to employ a self-taught form of meditation that helped him cope with the abuse by his parents. As he sat on the grass, he entered a deep level of spiritual awareness that had become more heightened than he had ever remembered. He soon became aware of an unknown presence. As he exited his meditative state, he immediately noticed a pair of intense red eyes staring back at him from across the alleyway.

The being was standing against the neighbor's white garage, about seventy feet from where MR was sitting. It was a thin black human shape that stood seven feet in height, when compared to the four-foot-high chained-linked fence at the end of his yard. There were wings folded on its back that extended above its long thin head. But those intense red eyes captured MR's concentration, to the point where he was literally paralyzed and frozen in place. The being was soon communicating with MR, in a telepathic form; more intent in garnering his attention than expressing information. The five-minute experience was suffused with an assortment of emotions, that ranged from tranquility to terror.

MR recognized that he was not dreaming or in a reflective state; that this was occurring in real-time. That was the moment where his perspective of the world around him changed forever.

He never forgot the encounter, and it influenced his life; though he was reluctant to disclose the incident until he started college and became part of an environment that would pay attention to what he had to say and not judge his experience. But MR still did not understand why he was the recipient of the winged humanoid's scrutiny. Then one evening, while he and his wife were watching a video, MR began to appreciate and grasp what had happened to him in 1981.

'The Mothman Prophecies' is a theatrical film that was released in 2002. It is based on John Keel's book by the same title, even though the movie never really captured the full intensity of the book or the actual events that occurred in Point Pleasant, WV in 1966-67. Nonetheless, the film gave an overall impression of the story and some of the narrative that Keel expressed in the book. MR told me that he was sitting at home watching the video, when the car accident scene unfolded. The winged being suddenly came into focus and MR instantly went into sheer panic and uncontrollably burst into tears.

His wife tried to comfort him, but he was beyond consolation. They continued to watch the video, but it was a terribly difficult experience for MR. Later that evening, he disclosed his boyhood encounter in detail with his wife. Since that time, he has not talked to anyone about the incident; until we talked today.

I would first like to state that my interview with MR was one of the most insightful I've experienced during my time as an investigator. We connected on a rare level, to the point where I could literally predict what he was going to say to me in each sentence. His experience confirmed to me that this phenomenon is not that of an indigenous being, but instead a flesh & blood extra-dimensional and/or extra-terrestrial entity that is either attracted to certain persons or summoned by specific forces. MR had no previous inclination of my theories, but rather defined what I have begun to believe during the investigation.

He also brought up, and totally discounted, the general speculation by many that this was a harbinger of future events. I asked MR if he thought that, while he was in a state of meditation, the being could have possibly been a self-manifesting thought-form. He believes, that in his case, the being sought him out because of the abuse he had suffered through his parents. As he began to read the recent sighting descriptions in the Chicago metro area, he formulated that there may indeed be more than one winged being and that many of the witnesses came upon it by happenstance. But he also feels that some of the encounters occurred because the being sought out the witness for a specific reason. MR didn't sense that the winged humanoid was evil but believes that it is an ancient being that has sought out others in the past, and that it is the venerable entity that people since have referred to as a 'demon.'

I forwarded my book, 'Mothman Dynasty: Chicago's Winged Humanoids,' to MR in the hope that he may offer more information on this being. I wanted him to read about the investigation that is detailed in the book, as well as understand the historical significance of this anomaly. It is my hope that MR's personal perspective may assist us in our continued desire to explain the winged humanoid phenomena.

OCTOBER 26, 2018 – ALSIP, IL

In November 2018 a report was submitted to Manuel Navarette of UFO Clearinghouse. The sighting took place on Friday October 26, 2018, at approximately 12:30 am. The report was submitted by an older couple who work as an over-the-road team for a trucking company in Alsip, IL. They both had been driving together for over 15 years and had been married for over 27 years. The gentleman was at the wheel of the truck when the encounter occurred, and his wife was in the passenger seat. Manuel spoke to both witnesses at a local restaurant near the truck yard in Alsip, IL.

Both agreed to have the story submitted but asked that their names be kept confidential due to the nature of their work and the fact that they did not want someone from their company (who was also based in Alsip, IL) to find out about their sighting.

The initial sighting report is as follows:

"We were on our way to park our truck at the yard after being on the road for two weeks. As we approached the railroad track crossing, we noticed something standing in the middle of the road and thought it was a homeless person walking along the tracks. We popped on the high intensity lights and to our surprise, it was not a homeless person at all. This thing looked like a large owl, as it had what looked like feathers and a flat rounded face with large eyes that reflected the LED lights on our truck. This thing appeared to lunge at us, while trying to cover its eyes with its left arm. I pulled on the airhorn and this thing turned its back on us and then took a couple of steps and then took off into the air and flew off into the night. We were left sitting there in complete shock as we watched it disappear into the night. After a minute or two of looking to see if the damn thing would come back around, we continued into the yard. We parked our truck and walked toward the car. As we approached our car, we heard what sounded like a scream followed by another and then silence. We hustled our tails to the car and left for home."

The area where the sighting took place is heavily industrialized with a few residential areas nearby. The railroad crossing mentioned sits approximately three quarters of a mile from the entrance and is surrounded by wooded area on West 122nd Street and is across the street from a Coca Cola plant. Manuel accompanied the couple to the location of the sighting. He attempted to garner permission from the landowner in order to place trail cameras at the location. Hopefully his effort will result in photographic evidence.

SUMMER 2010 NEAR ROCKFORD, IL

BACK IN AUGUST 2017, Tobias & Emily Wayland of The Singular Fortean Society (and members of Phantoms & Monsters Fortean Research) were contacted by a witness who claimed to have seen a creature comparable to the flying humanoid that had been haunting the area around Lake Michigan. The witness, who agreed to attach his first name, Dalton, reported his encounter that took place in 2010. This incident was the beginning of a string of reports in the area in and around Rockford, Illinois.

"If I had not experienced it firsthand, I would have probably dismissed it as fiction. Please, I assure you this is 100 percent the whole story of that night.

So, it began as a typical summer day approximately 5 years ago. These events take place in northern Illinois near Rockford. My friend, Nick, and I were cruising around in my 1997 Firebird. As the day progressed, we decided to head towards the country roads to do some drifting. Typical behavior for a 16-year-old with a sports car.

This was something that we did quite often also.

Jump ahead two hours or so, and it's around 11 pm and we are on a gravel road. We're in a location that was secluded but was farmland everywhere, so there were houses every so often. Now me and Nick are talking while I'm repeatedly slowing down and then applying the gas hard so I could get my vehicle sideways on this straight patch of road. The corn on the sides of this old gravel road were head height as it was towards the end of their growing season. Anyways, I began slowing down for probably the 5th time, only I could see the corn shaking. Nick and I both had stopped talking and were both watching the corn. I had expected a group of deer to run out and cross the road so naturally I slowed down to a slow roll. The corn was now shaking fiercely and quickly headed toward the road.

Now at this point we are staring at the corn waiting for the expected wildlife to pass. Now, I'm not sure how to describe this but what we saw was frightening. The corn parted about eight feet in front of my car, I don't know if you have ever seen a deer jump out of corn but it's like a horse hop. This thing was the size of big buck but was completely black. Mind you my headlights are focused right at the stretch of road and corn area, so the whole scene was well illuminated.

As it proceeded to jump out of the corn it opened a huge set of wings and remained airborne. It flew right in front of my car and did this zigzag flight pattern incredible fast. Almost like a fly or bug would do. After the quick zigzags it shot straight up into the air. I mean shot like it was placed in a canon and blasted in the sky.

My Firebird was a model that had T-tops, so we both jerked our heads up but due to my lights pointing forward obviously, and it being dark out, we couldn't see where the creature went. I floored my car, while Nick's screaming, "GO GO GO!" I drive as fast as I can while still maintaining control in the gravel. We drive for a good 15 minutes completely quiet. The whole time we were watching around us. I don't know why but we instantly assumed that the thing was chasing us. Now mind you that from the moment when we started to see the corn move to when the thing left our view was only a matter of maybe 30 seconds.

We finally start to calm down and were now on a road that was frequented more. We can see farmers in the fields on tractors. Being that I can see other people I feel safe. I decide to pull over on the side of the road and immediately say, "What the fuck was that!?" But we had no answers. The only thing we came up with was that it was the size of a deer but flew like a bat. We named it accordingly, 'The Deerbat.' We say it was the size of a deer but, in fact, it was humanoid shaped. It just ran out of the corn like a deer. The Deerbat was incredibly black like it was covered in tar.

After we stop talking, we notice in the field a couple yards by us is a "harvest in progress" sign. So again, being dumb teenagers, we decide to steal the sign. I run and grab it and shove it in the back seat and throw hoodies over it. It was a large sign and had the metal pole still attached to it. It didn't hide in the back of a Firebird very well. But we managed and we headed out of the country and made it to a neighboring town, New Milford. We both were thirsty and wanted a snack, so I pull into a gas station and back my car into a space that faces the main road. As soon as I shut my car off this old beat up rusted Chevy pulls in front of me as if he's blocking us in. His windows are tinted dark, we couldn't tell who was in it or what was going on. He remained there for several minutes. Just sitting. We didn't get out the car because this night was already a big nope, and the last thing I wanted was a hillbilly trying to start something. As mysteriously as he pulled up, without warning he drove off.

We assumed that it was somebody who seen us take the sign and that he was getting my plates. Maybe he was waiting for us to get out of the car to confront us. The only problem was that he entered from our left and exited on the right. He was never behind my car to get my plates I didn't have a plate on the front of my car. Anyways, he left so we went and got our drinks and chips and drove to my house.

I have no idea if the truck was related to any of the other

events of that night or not, but it was creepy, nonetheless. To me the only way I can describe the Deerbat is to compare it to the creature in the movies 'Jeepers Creepers.' That's exactly what we saw. Obviously though that's just a movie. I'm not religious, but this is how I picture a demon.

Jump ahead a month or so and I'm watching the show called Monster Quest, and they were focusing on a creature called Mothman. Instantly I freaked out all over again. This thing fits with what we saw, except for one detail. Witnesses describe glowing red eyes that pierce looks through you. We didn't see that. The Deerbat was completely black and was absent of light.

We never saw the Deerbat again and to this day we tell people about what we saw. They always ask the same question, 'what drugs were you on?' To be clear, I don't do drugs."

Tobias was able to interview Dalton about his experience, and his story remained largely unchanged from a previously published account.

According to Dalton, the entire sighting lasted between 15-20 seconds, and neither he nor his friend were able to discern any fine details about the creature's appearance.

"The thing arc jumped out of the cornfield but never landed,"
said Dalton. *"It zigzagged back and forth, like a bat."*
"There were no glowing red eyes," he continued. "It was just totally black. It was a big thing with big wings."
"It all happened so fast we couldn't get details."

He was able to recall that the winged being had four appendages in addition to its wings, although he's not certain if there were two arms and two legs, or if all four appendages were legs.

Dalton noted, too, that the fear he and his friend felt seemed like a "natural reaction to the situation," rather than any supernatural effect created by the creature.

SUMMER 2010 NEAR WEMPLETOWN, IL

ON TUESDAY, October 23, 2018, I received an email describing another and comparable winged being observed in the Rockford, Illinois area:

> "I just found out about the flying humanoid sightings around Chicago. In fact, I'm going to get the book and see if there is anything related to what I encountered in the summer of 2010.
>
> This took place in northern Illinois, not far from Rockford. My friend and I were just riding around in my car. As the day continued, we decided to head out towards the country backroads. We were both 17 and this was the summer before our senior year in high school.
>
> We had been riding around for several hours at night, and around 10 pm we are on a gravel road I wasn't familiar with. It was a location that had lots of farmland all around and a few houses here and there. We were talking while I'm speeding along this gravel road. There was no drinking or drugs involved. The corn on both sides of the road was high.
>
> I looked ahead and noticed that the road was about to dip, so I slow back. As I approached the dip, I could see the corn shaking to the right of me as the headlight hit it. We both stopped talking as we watched the corn. I thought it was probably deer about to sprint out onto the road, so I slowed down to a crawl. The corn was now shaking violently. We're staring at the corn waiting for the deer to jump out.

Then suddenly, the corn literally parts open just to the right of us. This 'thing' steps out. It was the size of a large man and all black. As it walked out of the corn it was well illuminated by my headlights.

It leaped and opened these huge set of wings, and instantly went airborne. It quickly flew right in front of my car and swooped up into the air as it reached the other side of the road. I swear, the first thing that came to my mind was the 'Jeepers Creepers' monster! I didn't see any facial features, but the wings were very wide and looked like that of a giant bat!

I floored the gas pedal. My friend was yelling to get out of there! I drove as fast as I could, trying to maintain control on the gravel surface. We drove for a good 5 minutes before saying a word.

The whole time we're looking around us, hoping that thing wasn't chasing us. We began to calm down and soon ended up on a road I knew. As I thought about it, that thing looked like it was covered in shiny black tar. It had a weird sheen to it. The fact that it accelerated into flight so quickly had me stumped. My friend and I talked about it through our entire senior year and never did have a clue as to what we saw. We referred to it as the 'Flying Tar Man.' We didn't dare tell anyone else at school. I recently told my wife about it, but she's a skeptic and doesn't believe in the supernatural.

Anyway, after I heard about the sightings around Chicago, I figured I'd track you down and write about it. I live in Texas currently.

Thanks for reading. Curt."

I called Curt to discuss the incident. This occurred in Winnebago County, north of Rockford, Illinois on a gravel farm road near Rt. 70. He said he believed it was somewhere near Wempletown. The description is very similar to the winged humanoids reported to us in 2017, and almost the exact scenario experienced by two previous witnesses. He told me that the height was about six foot, and that the body was very thin. He estimated that the wingspan was about fifteen foot. He also said that it had arms and legs. The 'Jeepers Creepers' reference was also used by several witnesses from the Chicago area as well. When Tobias Wayland read the report, he was sure that it was either the same witness he had talked to, or someone who created a copycat version of the event. After repeated conversations with Curt,

I'm positive that this was a separate encounter.

AUGUST 2004 NEAR ROCKFORD, IL

ON NOVEMBER 23, 2018, I received another report from the Rockford, IL area:

> "I recently learned of the Chicago humanoid sightings and then about the black winged humanoid sighting near Rockford, Illinois. This was shocking to me because I live in Winnebago County in a city (Loves Park) that borders Rockford which is sixty miles from Chicago. I have seen a similar black winged being.
>
> I was standing on the deck in my backyard late one summer evening, it was August of 2004, I was stargazing as I often do, when I was startled by the sudden furious barking of a neighbor's dogs. As I turned and looked towards the direction of the barking, it was at that moment, I saw an all-black seven-foot-tall man with huge bat-like wings flying across the park that borders my backyard. It then descended to

approximately five to six feet above ground. It pulled or folded its wings in slightly and then glided along the paved path that runs through the park. It continued gliding through an easement between two houses disappearing from my sight.

Stunned by what I had just seen I quickly ran in through the backdoor and out the front, stepped out onto the front porch and that is when I heard a loud screeching sound. The sound was so loud, and it was coming from the thick tree line across the street from the park on yet another easement.

I quickly stepped back into the house, shut and locked the door and woke my sleeping husband. I asked him to come listen to what I was hearing. I told him what had happened. The screeching continued sporadically for approximately five minutes. Then it went silent. The afternoon of the following day, after the incident as I was walking to the mailbox, the elderly neighbor who resided in the house that the tree lined easement borders the backyard yelled across the street asking me if I had a minute to take a look at something strange in his backyard. What the neighbor showed me was his chain link fence posts were bent down at a forty-five-degree angle. It was only the posts closest to the tree line. He was perplexed as to what could have possibly caused this to happen.

I attempted to explain to him what it was I saw and heard the night before. Just as I went into detail that I saw something very large and strange flying, I got a raised eyebrow with a strange look. He told that what I saw was a Heron and that no bird could have bent those posts like that. So, I quickly dropped the subject, as I walked back home another neighbor 2 houses away yelled, 'hey, did you hear all that loud weird noise last night? It woke me up. I thought the rain forest, or something moved in overnight.' To which I replied with 'yes I heard, and I have not a clue as to what it was.'

I researched for a few months after my encounter and

found out quite a bit about Mothman sightings. However, nothing out there matched what I saw that night. So, as time went by it had become all but a faded memory over the years until now. E.J."

This is the third account that we have received from Winnebago County, Illinois near Rockford. The incidents occurred between 2004- 2010, but also closely parallel the more recent sightings in the Chicago metro area and southern Wisconsin.

SUMMER 2017 – ROCKFORD, IL

I THEN RECEIVED a telephone call on November 27, 2018, that referenced a sighting from the same area. This was the fourth sighting within and around the city of Rockford, IL. This specific incident occurred in the late summer of 2017 around the same time many of the Chicago reports were coming forward.

The eyewitness 'KJ' stated it was approximately 6 am and that she was on the outside porch. Suddenly, she observed a human-like being walking in the yard of a house on the corner of Bruce St. and Woodlawn Ave. in Rockford, IL. (about one block away). The being suddenly produced a large set of wings and took flight, gliding over the back gate of the property. It then disappeared into the trees and foliage on the next block. There was enough morning light available for an excellent observation.

She had trouble comprehending what she had seen, and immediately went back inside the house to tell her boyfriend and his mother what she had seen. She described the being as tall and dark, almost black. The wingspan was very broad.

I was able to briefly talk to the witness about the incident.

She was apprehensive about coming forward, until she was told about the other reports in the Rockford area by a family member. She had no previous knowledge of the Chicago sightings.

SUMMER 1999 – ROCKFORD, IL

THEN ON NOVEMBER 29, 2018, I received a telephone call from an elderly woman ('SS') in Rockford, Illinois who witnessed a winged humanoid in 1999, along with her husband and a close friend.

The incident occurred during the summer, in the early evening when there was a full moon. The trio was relaxing on the friend's front porch, which was located on Willard Ave. W, near Auburn High School and Cottonwood Airport in Rockford.

During a conversation, the friend stopped talking and began to stare across the street. SS looked in the same direction, and noticed a dark gray winged humanoid slowly flying near a large tree. SS stated to me that it seemed like the being 'was in slow motion' as it glided toward the tree. The friend said, 'do you see that?' The witnesses were close enough to notice that it had small cat-like ears and intense red eyes. There were no other facial features visible. It was quite muscular throughout the body and had two defined legs and had arms that were attached to the wings.

She stated that the winged humanoid was seven foot in length with a wide wingspan. The wings were like those of a bat with a leather-like membrane. Apparently, the being briefing perched in the tree, but again took flight. This is when SS's husband took notice. The winged being was gliding towards a pair of large pine trees, as its legs were 'kicking up and down' while in flight.

The being flew between the two pine trees, and then suddenly 'vanished.' SS said, 'gargoyle,' and her friend acknowledged 'yes, a gargoyle.'

After the incident, SS stated that they seemed to have forgotten the encounter until a year later when she asked her friend if she remembered the sighting. Her friend said she had but had also forgotten the incident.

SS's son told her about the recent reports and suggested she call me. He was also aware of the winged humanoid sightings in the Chicago area.

This was the second sighting I had received of a winged humanoid which had suddenly vanished. The other sighting was in Chicago, a few blocks south from Wrigley Field.

Between January 19-22, 2019 I received a series of large winged being sightings in the Gary, Indiana area. The descriptions, in general, matched the previous sighting reports. Unfortunately, there were few details offered that would reasonably convince me that these were actual winged humanoids. I did make a note of the incidents and referenced each on the interactive map, if only for comparison to later reports.

DECEMBER 26, 2018 – PRAIRIE CREEK RESERVOIR, IN

I RECEIVED a telephone call from an eyewitness on January 23, 2019. 'TH' and his wife were traveling southbound on a county road, about a mile south of the Prairie Creek Reservoir near

Muncie, Indiana. The date was December 26, 2018, at dusk. A huge flying object caught TH's attention.

TH is a military veteran, hunter, trapper and farmer who lives in the immediate area. His knowledge of military flying craft, wildlife and his keen sense of observance was apparent while I talked to him. The winged being that he was observing was unlike anything he had ever seen before. The creature was flying just above treetop level and was easily visible to the witness. His reaction was to slam on his brakes in wonderment, exclaiming to his wife, 'do you see that?' His wife was shaken by the sudden stop and was unable to react fast enough to see the winged being.

TH stated that the being was humanoid in shape with an obvious 'face.' The body had a length of approximately six to seven feet, with bat-like wings that were extremely wide. The being was dark-colored and seemed to glide at a steady speed. He never noticed the flapping of wings while watching the creature.

TH's wife states that her husband has been truly affected by the incident and has constantly mentioned it to her, attempting to explain what this winged being really was. He had refused to mention the incident outside of his family. When TH read about the recent sightings in Gary, Indiana, he called his wife from his job and asked her to contact me right away. He later called me when he got home.

This witness was very forthcoming and anxious to find out what this creature was.

WINTER 2011 – PRAIRIE CREEK RESERVOIR, IN

ON JANUARY 27, 2019, I received an email that referenced a sighting, in response to my blog post about the large flying humanoid observed near Prairie Creek Reservoir, Indiana:

> "My husband was on Facebook and saw this article that you wrote and immediately showed it to me because I am certain this is the creature I saw eight years ago in 2011 around this same time of year (winter) when I was on my way to work.
>
> The events unfolded as such. I was driving down Road 1 in between 400 and 500 South. Now this location is in Randolph County just ten to fifteen minutes kind of east from Prairie Creek Reservoir. This is reason why the article caught my husband's attention.
>
> As I was driving, I saw what appeared to be a human crouched down in the road. As I got closer, I slowed down. It did not move, as I came to a complete stop. This thing slowly turned its head to look my way and it had greenish yellowish colored eyes, like the color of cat eyes. It stared for maybe 3 seconds and then proceeded to slowly get up from its position, like a human would stand up on their legs. It turned towards my car. It stepped on my car and used it to take off. Then it lifted off like a glider towards the sky. I turned my head just in time to see it tuck its legs into its body, so it did somewhat appear as a bird in flight. Its wingspan was wider than anything I've ever seen on an animal.
>
> I told my husband what had happened, and he told me it had to have been a bird. Now he's not so sure, since he's seen your article. I've never said anything to anyone else in fear that I would be made out to be an idiot. I also would still like to maintain my privacy as I do not want any public attention from this as I have a young daughter and do not want her to be bought into it either. I hope you'll maintain my privacy as well

and keep my involvement just a witness as you did the other witness in your article. RP"

SUMMER 2017 – PRAIRIE CREEK RESERVOIR, IN

It wouldn't be long before I received another report from the Prairie Creek Reservoir, IN area. The following email was forwarded to me on February 1, 2019:

"My mom sent me your article because I have also seen the humanoid at Prairie Creek Reservoir. I am originally from Muncie, IN and grew up spending a lot of time at Prairie Creek because my family has a boat there.

It was summer 2007 when we had taken a boat ride and watched the sunset. It was dusk and the sun was setting as we approached our dock. As we got closer my friend and I both saw what looked like a human standing at the end of our dock and thought it was strange because there was no one else around. Our neighboring boats were all docked and there were no other cars around. We were the only people out that evening from our dock area. This being then turned around and we saw the glowing yellow eyes. At this point, we were freaked out wondering what this was because there was something totally off about it and it was clearly not a normal human. Then, as we got even closer, it spread its wings, flapped a few times and soared up into the sky. It was way too big to be a bird. I've never seen anything like it before or after. It was probably around five to six feet tall and very dark in color. The whole body and wings were gray/black. AB"

The eyewitness was a well-known network media professional, so I believe that their account was very credible.

AUGUST 2006 – BENSENVILLE, IL

I RECEIVED a telephone call from an eyewitness who stated that he and his son observed a cape winged humanoid in Bensenville, Illinois.

The eyewitness 'Brian' said that one evening in August 2006 he and his adult son were sitting on the back porch of his home in Bensenville, Illinois. This location is a village that borders the southwest edge of O'Hare International Airport.

The eyewitness' neighbor has a large pine tree in the adjacent yard. Both Brian and his son were looking in that direction when a large dark being quickly 'dropped' to the ground from the tree and grabbed a squirrel with its talons. The squirrel was literally screaming during the attack. The dark being then quickly jettisoned up into the tree. Both witnesses could hear the being moving up the tree, but neither caught sight of it again.

Brian described the humanoid as having strong and long 'grasshopper-like' legs with muscular thighs. It seemed to have cape-like wings that were wrapped around the body. These wings were never unfurled. He estimates the height of the humanoid at six feet or so. There was no distinct head or eyes, but the overall size and form was too large to be any bird that the longtime resident has ever seen or heard described. Both witnesses were shocked at what they had seen. I asked about not getting a photo, which I was told that the event happened so quickly that they never had a chance to do so.

The witness decided to come forward after his elderly mother in Wisconsin read about the Chicago sightings and urged him to contact me. I believe that this is the first report to state that one of these winged humanoids had attacked an animal. This is also one of the better descriptions of the legs and talons on these beings.

SUMMER 2012 – INDIANAPOLIS, IN

ON JANUARY 31, 2019, I received an email from a witness in Indianapolis, Indiana:

"A friend of mine just sent me an article on a flying humanoid creature seen in Indiana. It was about a recent sighting of this thing. My girlfriend and I both witnessed this same creature about six years ago (summer 2012) while traveling I-465 north headed to the Indianapolis International Airport around 3 am.

The creature (Mothman) as we have been calling it, flew right in front of our windshield! It soared in between 2 buildings and came right in front of the van (taxi van - I was on a cab fare). It turned its head and looked right at us with little red eyes. It then flapped its wings one time and flew quickly to the left. The wings were so beautiful. I'll never forget how amazing they were. It was a bat-like winged being. You could almost see through his wings. You could see the veins from all angles of the wings and light that illuminated through them in the background. And I'll never forget the eyes. They were piercing and felt as if they looked right into my soul. It was an extremely very deep feeling.

And you know what funny thing was? Even though this massive thing flew so close in front of the van and that I felt I was going to hit him, I never once put my brakes on. I think back about that a lot. I mean I'm a taxi driver with a chauffeur license trained to be safe and cautious.

Yet I never once slammed on my brakes or attempted to stop.

I just thought I should contact you. I hope to hear back from you. I would like to know more about this thing. We wanted to tell someone more well-known than just our circle of friends and family, but we didn't know who. CJ"

I contacted CJ for additional information. She and her companion (who was seated in the front) were with two fares (a soldier and his girlfriend in the back). CJ states that the winged being had a thin seven foot tall body, brownish in color. The bat-like wingspan was at least twelve feet in width. The red eyes had a distinct illumination and were very bright.

The area around the Indianapolis International Airport is well-known for UFO and anomalous activity.

FEBRUARY 9, 2019 NEAR CLAYTON, MI

I LATER RECEIVED an email on February 12, 2019, from a witness in southeast Michigan:

"I recently Googled 'Michigan cryptids' in order to find any information on what I saw fly across the sky on my way to work this past Saturday. I stumbled upon your website and the sighting from the person in Lansing, MI. So, I decided to give you my account of what I saw.

On Saturday 2/9/19 at around 10:30 pm I was driving into town on my way to work. I saw a dark figure the size of an adult human leap from a tree and fly across the sky and then over the road. I slammed on my brakes and watched this massive creature fly into a nearby wooded area. I tried to get pictures but because it was dark and this creature appeared to be jet black in color, nothing was visible in the photos. I live in Clayton, Michigan and work in Adrian and where I saw this creature was about halfway between the two towns. Which are only a twenty-minute drive apart. This is in southeast Michigan about a thirty-minute drive from the Michigan/Ohio State line so if we are all seeing the same creature then it is surely migrating. Name withheld"

I contacted the witness, who added a few minor details to his statement.

Artwork Credit: Donie Odulio

3

A BIGFOOT WITH WINGS?

FEBRUARY 22, 2019 – WOODSTOCK, IL

On February 23, 2019, I receive emails from the wife of the eyewitness who I'll refer to as 'TM'. I was later able to talk to TM by telephone on 2/24/19:

"Hello - my husband was returning home last night (Feb. 22nd - approx. 8 pm) from a trip to Walgreens. While driving home, he saw something eight to nine feet tall running across the road from the DuField Pond entrance on Country Club Road in Woodstock, Illinois. He said it was approximately one third the width of the road and part of it looked leathery, though he wouldn't call it leather exactly.

He is interested in speaking to you about it, but this afternoon he didn't seem ready to talk. I've asked him if he could sketch what he saw before he forgets. He indicated he's not going to forget this.

Just wanted to give you a heads-up and wondered if you have received any other reports in the Woodstock, IL vicinity."

I subsequently received the following email after I made my inquiry:

"Hi Lon - he said he will call you tomorrow if that's okay. I was home when this happened, so I didn't see anything. All I know is I believe my husband. I did go out to DuField this morning because we've had snow/ice/slush. I wanted to see if I could find any traces of whatever this was. There were a lot of tracks and prints near the entrance, though mostly boot prints. Some did not look like boots. However, it was hard to tell. I took photos and videos of the area."

I then talked to TM, who stated that he was driving on Country Club Rd. near the entrance to the Dufield Pond Conservation Area in Woodstock, IL. Suddenly, a large biped ran out onto the road approximately thirty feet ahead of him and quickly crossed to the opposite side. He said that he thought that it may have been a Bigfoot initially, but then noticed that it had a large set of membrane wings attached to the back, extending over the top of its head. He described the shape of the wings as that of a gargoyle. The body was eight to nine feet in height and covered in dark fur. The arms and legs were well defined. He didn't notice any facial features. TM got an excellent look at the creature since his headlights illuminated it and the light from the conservation area backlit it as well.

He also stated that he had felt like it was a warning or harbinger of some kind. He did mention 'Nephilim' when discussing the encounter. It had upset him and that he was unable to talk about it until the next day.

I later received a sketch and a statement from TM's wife:

"The sketch is attached. It is more of an outline. The yellow at the bottom represents his headlights. The yellow at top is the

light at the DuField entrance. DuField conservation is a pond. Not sure if these things are attracted to water?"

I contacted Tobias & Emily Wayland and asked them to follow-up with TM. They later interviewed the witness and conducted an on-site investigation.

FEBRUARY 25, 2019 NEAR DARIEN, WI

ON FEBRUARY 25, 2019, I received a telephone call from an eyewitness 'NV' who stated she had observed a winged being early that morning at around 5:30 am near Darien, Wisconsin.

NV was traveling west on Creek Rd. on her way to work. As she approached the Turtle Creek bridge, she observed a large winged being that she described as a 'flying witch.' The being was at a tree-top altitude and was gliding in her direction. It was early dawn, but there was enough available light for NV to make out a form.

The winged being suddenly descended towards NV's car and barely missed colliding with the hood. NV stated that the being's wingspan was much wider than her car and that the body was a brownish color, like a 'paper bag.' The body looked feminine and slight. The wings were bat-shaped and very large. She never noticed the wings flapping. The speed in which it descended was 'not natural.' The face was unremarkable, almost 'blank.' NV noted that she swerved and almost hit the guard rail.

NV did not notice where the winged being flew to after the encounter. NV is of Hispanic descent and stated that the being reminded her of a 'witch' that was described to her as a child. NV was quite upset and worried that she may encounter this being in the future. March 7, 2019 – Woodstock, IL

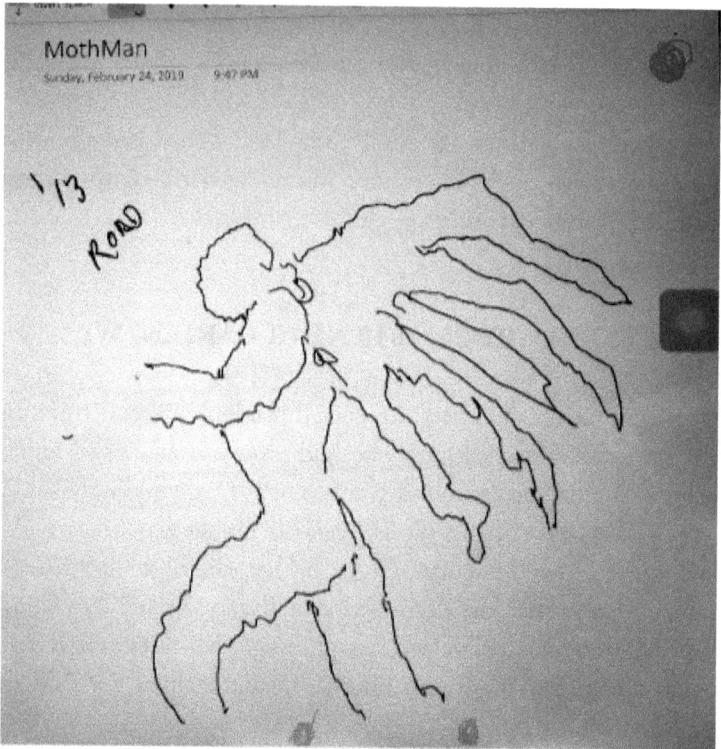

On March 22, 2019 I received an email that mentioned another sighting of a large winged biped in Woodstock, Illinois on Thursday, March 7th, 2019:

> *"My daughter saw this on Rose Farm Rd in Woodstock, IL while driving home. It ran in front of her car. She is extremely freaked out right now. She described it as extremely tall with fur and large wings. She said that when she saw it, she had an overwhelming sense of fear and dread. I hope this helps with your investigation. KS"*

The witness was reluctant to comment beyond the initial

report, mostly out of fear. The local media was also causing some unwanted excitement in the community as well. I simply refused to cooperate with the local media because of the sensation they had created.

FEBRUARY 28, 2019 – WOODSTOCK, IL

IN THE MEANTIME, Tobias Wayland was contacted by a man who said that he had seen an 'unusual being' with wings and 'bright green eyes' that charged at him from the McHenry County Fairgrounds in the early morning hours of February 28, 2019. The witness compared his encounter to a sighting that had been reported in Woodstock earlier in the month.

According to a message received through the Singular Fortean Society's contact page, the witness stated:

> "I was outside Jewel Osco in Woodstock, Illinois and believe to have seen the same visual of an unusual being in the McHenry County Fairground. It screeched at me then charged the fence, about thirty feet from the fence. It had very bright green eyes and had wings. It was all black in color and leathery. It ran back towards the woods in the McHenry County Fairgrounds. I called the Woodstock Police Department and they had county sheriffs respond to the location."

Tobias attempted to contact the witness by telephone at a predetermined time that was agreed to by all parties but was forced to leave a voicemail. The witness did not yet respond.

A Freedom of Information Act (FOIA) request for any information pertinent to the incident was then filed with the

McHenry County Sheriff's Office, and while an official report was not written, the 911 call information was released.

According to the incident detail report documenting the call, at 2:46 am on February 28, 2019, an officer responded to the 911 call of a man who said he'd seen a 'mysterious creature described as being seven to eight feet tall and wearing all black' that 'charged at him from the fairgrounds screeching at him while he was in the Jewel lot. It then retreated.' The witness named the creature the Dufield Pond Swamp Monster, since he had the first sighting with police involvement.' The report then stated that the, 'investigation to continue.'

APRIL 20, 2014 – WAUCONDA, IL

Tobias soon after received an eyewitness account that he later published on The Singular Fortean Society website:

On April 20, 2014 Paula was sitting near a window in the bedroom of her ground-level apartment near the Lakewood Forest Preserve in Wauconda when she saw a bright beam of light "come shooting down" across the street at around 11 p.m.

"It was so bright and defined," said Paula.

The light, which lasted between fifteen to twenty seconds, was an orange/gold color and did not illuminate its surroundings; nor did it move much, making only a slight "side-to-side or back-and-forth" motion.

The light retracted at one point, only to reappear a moment later. Paula fell back onto her bed in shock.

"Oh my god, this thing sees me!" she remembers thinking. "I had the deepest feeling this thing saw me, it knows."

But the light retracted a final time and was gone.

"I heard a hum at the end, just before it took off," said Paula.

Two years later, in 2016, also on April 20, Paula encountered a terrifying winged being in the same area. She was taking the garbage out just before 6 a.m. when something drew her eye from across the street. In the early morning gloom, she saw a huge, winged being.

Paula described the being as perhaps seven to eight feet tall when standing erect, but it carried itself hunched over, limping along. It was completely black, and from what she could see its upper body and head were covered in hair. The being had long, leathery wings which were partially wrapped around its body as it moved towards Paula; jumping forward similarly to watching someone move through a strobe light. The terrifying creature made an unnatural groaning noise as it advanced.

Paula felt a palpable sense of evil emanating from the bat-winged monster.

"This is evil," she recalled. "I'm seeing evil."

Fearing for her safety, she quickly turned to flee back into her apartment. After fumbling with her keys for a moment, she opened the door and turned around, terrified that the creature might be right behind her—but it was gone.

Paula said that she only knew a few of her neighbors personally, and unfortunately the ones she knew had not witnessed either event; although one of her neighbors with whom she was friends did take her encounters seriously.

"I don't know what to say," Paula said of her experiences. "But I know what I saw."

SPRING 2010 – JOLIET, IL

ON APRIL 4, 2019 I received an email from a witness in Joliet, Illinois:

"I believe I may have seen one of those winged humanoids about ten years ago in Joliet, IL. It was about 2:00 am near the end of March or the beginning of April. I was watching TV with the window open slightly. I kept hearing a muffled cry, almost like a woman crying in the distance. I finally decided to look out the window and then go to back door to see what it was. I was looking all over the backyard and neighboring yards but didn't see anything. When I was about to give up, I heard it again. I noticed that it was coming from above me. I looked up and noticed something about four feet tall sitting on the peak of the house behind me. I grabbed my phone to take a picture but when I was about to take the photo it turned its head to look at me. It scared the crap out of me. Then it dropped like it fell. Right before it hit the ground its wings came out and it swooped away. I couldn't believe how big the wingspan was. DG"

I talked to DG by telephone the next day. He believed it was the early spring of 2010 in the area of County Rd. and Black Rd. in west Joliet, Illinois. DG states he heard what sounded like a woman crying at around 2 am local time. After a while, he looked out the back door and noticed a four to five foot dark colored entity perched on the peak of his neighbor's roof. The being was crouched down and reminded DG of a gargoyle. He grabbed his phone to take a photo but was instantly halted when the being looked in his direction. DG said he didn't see the eyes, but 'knew' it was looking at him and that he was terribly frightened. In fact, he dropped his phone in shock.

The winged being stood and leaped from the roof, then dove towards the ground. As it descended, the huge wings unfurled as it swooped upwards and quickly ascended into the night sky. DG never saw the wings flap as the being ascended.

He did notice that it had pointed ears but could not make out any further features on the face.

The wings were attached from the shoulders to the legs and did not seem to have detached arms.

DG contacted me after hearing my live interview with Mancow on WLS Radio in Chicago. Joliet, Illinois is approximately forty-five miles southwest of Chicago.

AUGUST 2018 – HAMMOND, IN

ON AUGUST 12, 2019 I received an email and then a telephone call from Mark Hagan of the South Shore Ghostbusters. He wanted to report a sighting of a large winged humanoid in the Hammond, Indiana area, which occurred August 2018:

"It was August of 2018. My wife and I were driving south on Calumet Ave. and were coming up to the red light at 131st St when we heard what sounded like leather rustling. We looked to the retention pond to our left and saw glowing red what I am going to assume were eyes and saw a large bat-like creature take to the skies. It was dark colored and easily had to be about six feet or more tall from what I could make out. Wingspan was close to ten feet or more.

About a week or so later I was driving with my colleague in the South Shore Ghostbusters. This time we saw the same creature atop the Cline Ave. overpass. It looked like it was eating something. We turned around only to see it take off to the skies once more.

We have been investigating the area and found that this creature sticks close to the water. We have heard multiple accounts of seeing red glowing lights over the waters of the Lost Marsh since June or so of this year."

Hagan told me that he is very familiar with the large fowl in the area, and that this being was not one of the indigenous birds known to inhabit the areas around Lake Michigan.

These sightings were comparable in location and description from a report made to us on July 1, 2017. Any subsequent reports from this general area would be of great value to our investigation.

SUMMER 2003 – ALSIP, IL

ON SEPTEMBER 2, 2019, I received another report of an owl-like humanoid in the Alsip, Illinois area:

"I recently came across your article on the Chicago Owlman. I, along with another witness, have seen this creature, or one similar. This was sometime in 2003. We were quite young at the time. This was in Alsip, IL, right by the intersection of 128th Pl and Cicero. I even have screenshots of when I casually brought up the encounter again in 2015 to the other witness to corroborate. We both remember the encounter vividly.

I had only a silhouetted view, but I can best describe the creature as large, about the size of a large human man. Massive wings that it held up in a defensive/pre-flight posture out from its sides, and a human-like head that seemed to have no distinguishable features, save for two very large, almost glowing yellow owl-like eyes.

The creature sifted through the hedge bushes and came up to the bay window of the room we were occupying, making a loud noise as it slammed/pressed its body up against the window, its eyes staring right at us in the room. This creature nearly took up the entire bay window's space, and it stayed there once it hit the window, unlike an owl if it had accidentally flown into it. It was no regular owl. Much too large, as the silhouette was massive, and the eyes were the size of baseballs.

Being young, my friend and I quickly vacated the room in terror and alerted my sleeping father who immediately searched the perimeter of the house, yet nothing was found.

I nearly teared up reading your witness accounts on the website as it struck very close to home for me, as the image is still burned into my mind to this day.

If you need any more information, don't hesitate to contact me at any time. My experience has been a huge point of interest in my mind ever since it happened, and I would love nothing more than to assist you in your investigation in any way. LA"

I contacted the witness by telephone and received the following updates. It seems this incident occurred in the summer of 2003. LA was very credible in her description of the event, including the emotions and reactions by both her and the friend. They both remember the details of the incident, which left an indelible impression with both witnesses. This is the second 'Owlman' sighting/encounter reported in the Alsip, IL area. The other reported incident occurred more recently on Friday, October 26, 2018.

SEPTEMBER 27, 2019 – BARRINGTON, IL

THE FOLLOWING encounter account was posted on Reddit on Sept. 29, 2019. I followed up with the witness and later talked to her by telephone:

"I am so happy I stumbled onto this sub! This happened two days ago and I'm still so confused. I was driving home from work on a bright, sunny day. I live in a wooded area on Northern Illinois about an hour outside of Chicago. I get about a mile from my house. As I'm making my way down an unoccupied street, this creature runs in front of my car about 2 car lengths in front of me. It was a bat-like creature of some sort. I could clearly make out the shape of bat wings. But it wasn't flying. It was running like a gorilla. It would extend its wings out in front of itself and push itself forward, just like a gorilla does when it runs at full force. This thing was also a flat dark black in color. It was at least half the size of my dog, who is a seventy pound Pitbull/ Boxer mix. I tried to search for giant bats in the area and I found some sightings of giant bats flying over Chicago over the last two years. I've also found some references to the Mothman and the Jersey Devil, but I don't think this thing was as big as a man. And none of the stories I've read mention these giant bats running. However, I did learn that vampire bats are the only species of bats that run. And based on videos of vampire bats running, this creature moves in a very similar manner. So, now I'm nervous about letting my dog out alone. Any theories are appreciated. KE"

I contacted KE through the message portal and then talked to her by telephone. Her description to me was that this being was jet black and the size of a human toddler. The wigs were outstretched with attached claws, comparable to a bat. It ran across the street very quickly. She did not get a look at the head but said that the body was bat-like but more streamlined. The legs were long and resembled a canine's hocked leg with clawed feet.

This encounter in Barrington, Illinois. The witness had just turned onto Meadow Hill Rd. from W. County Line Rd when she noticed the creature cross the road in front of her. Could this have been a juvenile winged humanoid? It is an intriguing account.

OCTOBER 5, 2019 – RICHMOND, IL

On October 15, 2019 I received a winged humanoid sighting report from Richmond, Illinois:

"On Friday October 5, 2019 around 10 pm my 17-year-old son and I were coming home through Richmond, Illinois. He wanted McDonald's. We took the backroads home (we live in Wisconsin on border) and on Rt 173 and Broadway we both saw something very tall (six to seven feet) hunched over with the brightest red eyes we've ever seen! It looked as if it were floating or hopping. We couldn't make out much as it was very dark, but it was not like any animal we've seen before! When I got home, I Googled animals and found some Mothman myth. I'm not sure what we saw but it was out of the ordinary. We take this road often but only a few times at night and had never seen this before. It was maybe ten to twenty feet from our car and my son was freaking out telling me to 'go,' so we didn't stop. Our family thinks we're crazy and teases us saying we saw a zombie, so I'd prefer this to stay anonymous. I came across your info and thought I'd share. We didn't notice any wings, but it was very dark. We both thought it was hopping like a kangaroo and now I'm

curious if there are any other odd sightings in this area. MO"

I was later able to talk by telephone to 'MO.' She had left work late on Friday, October 5, 2019, and had picked up her 17-year-old son on the way home. The time was approximately 10 pm. They on Rt. 173 (Kenosha St.) and Broadway Rd. on their way to a McDonalds. They were also adjacent to the North Branch Conservation Area.

They both noticed a pair of very bright red eyes along the side of the road. The creature was about seven feet in height and dark in color. It was stooped or hunched over, as if something heavy was attached to its back. The witnesses never saw wings, but it seemed some structure was on its back. As they approached it, the creature looked at them and started to 'hop' back. They had gotten very close to it, about twenty feet or less. As it hopped back towards the field, they looked back, and it seemed that it suddenly disappeared. It never took flight. OM stated that the eyes looked like two very bright lights that emanated from within the creature.

OM wanted to turn around and look again, but her son was totally freaked out by the encounter and insisted she continue driving. The witness had no knowledge of the winged humanoid sightings in and around Chicago. She immediately began to research her sighting and found my information.

4

O'HARE INTERNATIONAL AIRPORT / ROSEMONT

OCTOBER 5, 2019 – ROSEMONT, IL

In early October 2019, a witness eventually contacted me by email and by telephone after filing his initial report with MUFON; which resulted in an undesirable discussion with the field investigator. He then searched Google and found my contact information. His first email to me is as follows:

"I recently had a sighting of a black creature that flew off on Saturday, October 5 in Rosemont, Illinois. I reported the sighting to MUFON and was contacted by an investigator who demanded that I talk to him. I advised him that I did not want to talk to him and that I wanted to remain anonymous about this sighting. He then demanded that if I did not talk to him, that I would need to meet him in person to discuss the report and that he would have to take pictures and discuss the report in order for him to give it validity. I felt very pressured to make myself available for the investigator and that he had no interest in my privacy as I had previously requested. I told

him that I went to extraordinary measures to ensure that my name or picture would not find itself all over the internet. I explained to him that I only took up doing ride-share to provide extra income for my family and I did not want to have my information or my family's information posted all over the place for people to ridicule.

After emailing back and forth with the MUFON investigator, I decided to look elsewhere for someone to report my sighting to who was going to respect my request for privacy. I just want to tell my story and then get on with my life. After looking around Google, I came upon your map and then your website and that's what leads to my email today. I can copy and paste the text of my sighting to you and am available to speak via email to you, but I do not want to meet in person nor be in any photographs.

I am not some kook who is seeing things and I have many, many more things to do than prank websites with made-up stories. I saw what I saw and remember it as clear as it had happened five minutes ago. Honestly how could you ever forget something like that. I am available in the afternoon and early evening when I ride-share. During the day I am usually at work and can only talk during my lunch break or during my breaks. I do not wish to talk to the MUFON investigator anymore and if you are associated with MUFON, then I will have to respectfully decline speaking with anyone as they did not respect my wish to remain anonymous."

After gaining the witness' trust, we eventually communicated freely. The following is a more detailed description of the incident and being:

"The encounter was so brief, but I also got a pretty good look at the creature. I was parked by the light pole. It allows me to

park a little more off the road. I was fumbling around with some charging cables that lead to the backseat of the car, for my passengers to use while in the car. I had my passenger side windows down to give my A/C a break.

It was then that I saw movement and looked up to see the creature emerging out of the trees. It was large and about six to seven feet tall. It was human-like in appearance, but almost solid black. There were no real features on this thing, just solid black. It swiveled its head around, looking and scanning and that is when I saw the glowing red eyes. The rest of the body was thin. I remember making note that it looked like a thin person and it was sort of hunched over, because its arms were down to about its knees. The wings were about as wide and it was tall, so about six to seven feet in width and looked like the wings of a bat. When it walked it kind of had a weird sort of a waddle, not so much like a penguin but like the kind of stride that a large bird (like an Emu) would have.

It stood there for a few seconds looking around, I know I'm not the only one who saw it because there must have been three to four other drivers there waiting for the next call. It unfurled its wings and after a few seconds it began to flap them, slow at first then faster and faster as it leaped into the air. It flew like a large bird would. It used its wings to gain altitude, slowly adjusting itself into a more normal stance. The sounds of the wings were kind of muffled but could still be heard for a few seconds. I will tell you something that I didn't tell the other investigator. In the moment it emerged from the trees, there was a strong smell of ammonia. It smelled like the old ammonia products that they used to use to clean the bathroom. It was very pungent but not overwhelming. When it took off the smell was gone within a minute of two. It took off in a south direction, headed toward the giant inflatable building that houses the indoor golf range.

Have there been reports of this thing recently?

The one question I do have for you is about the previous MUFON investigator. Why the pushy and aggressive posture toward me. It made me feel like he thought I was lying or trying to profit from this in some way?

Thank you and if you have any other questions, please contact me with them."

Manuel Navarette went to the location in order to video record the specifics of the report. At that time, we had little idea of how significant this sighting would be.

OCTOBER 18, 2019 – ROSEMONT, IL

ON OCTOBER 28, 2019, Manuel contacted me about a report that he had just received:

"On October 19, 2019, we were staying at the Edward Hotel in Rosemont, Illinois for a wedding we were attending that was being held at the hotel. During the reception and dance, I stepped outside to smoke a cigarette and get away from all the noise for a few minutes. I took a walk toward the parking lot smoking and checking my phone when I heard a loud scream. It sounded like a woman screaming so I looked up in the direction of where the scream was coming from hoping it wasn't really a woman in danger. Next to the parking lot is a large field with some trees but mostly a large vacant lot. I used my cell phone's flashlight to light the way and saw nothing except darkness. I walked over to the gravel path between the

parking lot and the field, toward where my car was parked. That is when I heard wings flapping and something flew right over the top of me, about maybe seven to ten feet above me. I could have easily thrown a rock and hit it as it flew over me and away.

This thing was at least six feet tall and was solid black with large wings. It looked like a giant-sized bat as it flew over me. It was all black and kind of stuck out against the lights of the parking lot and the lights from around the area including the gas station across the street. Three other people saw it as well, including a couple who were walking across the parking lot as I heard them exclaiming about it. It flew toward the expressway and the BP gas station. The entire time it was screeching loud and flapping its wings hard like it was trying to gain height. When I lost sight of it, it was about the height of the billboard across the street still shrieking away.

Now I know I had been drinking during the wedding and was a little buzzed when I walked outside, but I was as sober as a judge after seeing this thing. It was unnatural and was pretty much the scariest thing I ever did see, but I know for a fact that I saw it and those other people saw it."

Manuel noted that he spoke to the witness over the weekend by telephone. The witness states that he and his girlfriend were attending a mutual friend's wedding reception when he decided to step outside and smoke a cigarette. He stated when he first heard the screaming, it sounded almost like a woman in distress which make him look around to see if anyone needed help. He stated that as he walked along the gravel path, smoking and looking around and that is when he heard flapping sound. The witness said is sounded like when geese flap their wings only louder and deeper. It was then that he saw the entity fly over his head at a height of about seven feet above his head. He said the creature was solid black, but still reflected light from the street lamps in the parking lot and the surrounding area. He stated that it looked like a giant bat, that there was no other way to describe what it looked like. When asked if he saw any red eyes or other distinguishing features, the witness stated that he did not.

The witness states that it was moving too fast for him to pick out any features other than the general description he gave. He did confirm that there were at least three other witnesses who saw the entity when it flew over the parking lot, but he did not talk to them. I asked him to describe the sound and he said it was a cross between a woman screaming and an animal growling. When asked what kind of animal, he stated it sounded like a mountain lion.

The witness did say that the creature did gain altitude very quickly and when it faded out of sight, it was over the nearby expressway and about the height of the billboard it had passed. The entity was still making the screeching noise and could still be heard as it went out of sight. When asked about flight characteristics, the witness did add that the creature had two short legs that extended straight behind it in flight, therefore making it look like a bat in flight.

When asked what he did after the sighting, he said he went back inside and told his girlfriend who dismissed it as him seeing a crane or other large bird. They rejoined the reception and the rest of the night was uneventful. When asked if he had tried to take video or a photograph, the witness said that he was in shock and that he did not reach for his phone.

OCTOBER 28, 2019 – ROSEMONT, IL

THEN DURING THE first week of November 2019 our investigative team began to examine a report that was first forwarded to Manuel Navarette. Because of the extreme nature of this incident, several questions remain unanswered.

The following email is the initial report that was received. I have redacted the personal information and specific locations:

"I'm very hesitant to write to you with what I saw but the more I think about it, the more I have to tell someone about it. My name is (REDACTED) and I live in Rosemont, Illinois on (REDACTED). I have been living in Rosemont most of my adult life and I work in a nearby suburb as an (REDACTED). One of the perks of living where I live is that there is a (REDACTED) nearby and I can take walks to the park, sit down and escape for a little while. I enjoy taking walks at night when I am usually alone and can lose myself in my thoughts.

On that night, I could not sleep and decided to take a walk and sit for a few minutes in the cold. I thought that maybe that would bring about the urge to sleep and I could come back and get ready for bed. I put on my jacket and step outside and (REDACTED). As I step across (REDACTED), I notice that the area seemed strangely quiet, even with two expressways nearby. Mind you, I did not expect to hear crickets and such with the cold but the whole vibe seemed a bit off.

I sat at the usual place and I had not been there for more than five minutes when I saw the strangest thing. It looked like a very tall man standing by the (REDACTED), but the man was unusually tall and very thin. The man was standing next to what looked like a smaller man who seemed also very frail and thin but whose head was disproportionate to his body. They seemed to be conversing, but I could not hear anything from where I was sitting. As I watched them, a pair of women walked up to them and just stood there, almost as if they were in a daze. The tall person then did something that just shook me to my core and it was then that I realized that I should not have been there at that moment. The tall gentleman unfurled what looked like huge wings and stretched them out and then tucked them back in as the women approached. The smaller man then turned to the two women and that is when the area was bathed in bright (blue) light. The light only lasted at the very most one to two seconds and then only the tall winged being remained. The being then unfurled his wings and walked away from the waterfall, took a step or two while flapping his wings and took off. I watched it fly away and it reminded me how a goose would fly, low and steadily gaining speed. I remained where I was, and it was almost a full minute before I took a breath and tried to wrap my head around what I had just seen. To tell you the truth I was almost afraid to leave that (REDACTED) and make the walk back home, but when I did leave I almost sprinted back home and only felt secure when I shut the main door behind me and made my way upstairs to my apartment.

I do not know what I saw. I have no explanation for what I witnessed and there is no way I can describe it to anyone. I am certain that I was at the wrong place at the wrong time and I pray to God that I was not noticed. Whatever the result of this report, I had to get it off my chest and tell someone about what I saw that night and hope that someone will believe me and not think that my cheese has slipped off of my cracker. J"

I contacted 'J' and received the following email:

"Thank you for getting in touch with me so quickly. Manuel did speak to me about you and Tobias and he praised your professionalism and highly recommended you both. I do a lot of after hours volunteering (REDACTED) so during the week it's hard for me to talk on the phone. I can answer emails because I'm able to during work when I'm in front of my computer. This is something I don't want to talk about within (REDACTED) but I can speak with you and the other investigators when I'm home and have time.

I do have a question that I want to ask you about pertaining to dreams. Starting on the night after this incident occurred, I started having extremely lucid dreams. I would find myself in a brightly lit room and something telling me that I'm going to be fine. Then a 'hand' reaches out and touches my arm, then things go black and I wake up.

I'm not terrified but I am concerned. The dream has come to me four times already and each time it's the same thing.

This never occurred to me before but since that night it's been happening more and more. Could this be related? Any help would be greatly appreciated. J"

Not long after I received the previous email, 'J' sent another:

"I just had a very strange occurrence happened to me and (REDACTED). I went to lunch and as I was putting my trash in the receptacle, I was approached by a gentleman who said he was an investigator. He said he wanted to speak to me regarding what I saw. The man insisted that I speak with him and that he was an investigator who was trying to sort out what it was I had seen and reported. I asked him what organization he was with and how did he know who I was.

The gentleman only answered that he was an investigator and that it was imperative that I speak with him about what I saw. The man gave me a very bad vibe and I did not want to speak to him. My coworker, who was with me, had gone to the restroom and this is when the gentleman approached me and *insisted that I talk to him. I told him that I had already spoken with investigators and again asked him who he represented, and he only answered again that he was an investigator. My friend returned from the restroom and the man walked away without another word.*

This incident kind of shook me up and left me with even more questions than before. By any chance did any of you send an investigator to speak with me and how did you know where I was going to be for lunch?

I'm more than willing to talk but being approached in such a way in public and out of the blue just does not jive with me. I have had instances in the past where I've been stalked by an obsessive ex-boyfriend and it left me traumatized and a little jumpy and to have somebody approached me out of the blue and insistently ask me to speak with him kind of raised a lot of red flags for me. J"

I assured 'J' that we had not contacted any other individuals in reference to her report. I again asked if she would be willing to talk to me on the telephone or meet one of the team in person. I received the following response:

"Thank you for getting back to me. I don't want you to take this the wrong way, but I do not want to talk about this anymore.

All sorts of strange things have been happening to me since the day that gentleman tried to talk to me. I have been plagued by numerous calls. When I pick-up I hear nothing on the other side. I also have been followed and I've had people who do not belong in my neighborhood or at my job sitting there watching me. All this started after I had this sighting. I don't know what it was that I saw but it seems that I was not meant to see it and now I'm scared something's going to happen to me. I have even considered purchasing a handgun just to protect myself.

I'm not crazy and I know what I saw was real. I saw it with my own two eyes but now I'm being stalked and have people coming up to me and asking questions who I don't even know. Now people are calling and trying to intimidate me and frankly it's working. I have had little sleep since this has happened and my nerves are completely frazzled. I can't do this anymore. I don't care if people don't believe me or think I'm crazy but I know what I saw and now it seems like people want me to keep my mouth shut or they want to probe into what and who I am because of this incident.

I know you get probably hundreds of reports today dealing with all sorts of paranormal stuff and I'm just one person who saw one incident. But apparently it stirred up a hornet's nest and now I'm caught in the middle. It's nothing against you, but I'm scared, and I want this to stop. J"

After I received this last email, I tried to assure 'J' on the importance of her testimony. I explained the history of the winged humanoid sightings in the area and that her encounter was unique. I also explained my background and how I have worked with hundreds of experiencers over the past forty years. I wanted to gain her confidence and have her calmly recall to me what she observed that evening. I received the following email a few days later:

"Lon, It happened at (REDACTED). I was sitting at the (REDACTED). I go there to get away and relax. I was facing the (REDACTED) when I saw them.

I was sitting there, just relaxing in order to decompress so I could fall asleep.

I was only there about five minutes when I saw them standing there. I did not hear anything, but it looked like they were talking. They continued this for about 1 minute before the two women showed up and they disappeared. The women looked completely normal, they walked up and just stood there like they were in a trance and then the bright blue light came out of nowhere and they were gone. The winged one then took off and was gone within ten to twelve seconds of the others disappearing.

After the winged one left, the place was quiet, just like a normal night. I quickly left and went back home. Since that night I have had very lucid dreams and the latest one was last night. I saw the smaller being and it looks like a typical (Grey) alien. In three dream it tells me that, 'everything is going to be fine and that you are perfectly safe and will be spared.' That's where the dream ends.

Lately I have had a bad feeling of dread which is so not like me since I'm usually happy and talkative. I feel like something horrible is about to happen. I can't shake this feeling and other people have started to notice a change in my demeanor.

I don't know how much else I can provide as that's all I remember, and I hope it helps you with your investigation. I just don't want something to happen to me or somebody I love, and things are starting to get a little too strange and scary for me.

I don't know how much else I can help you. You have been nothing but kind and respectful I appreciate that wholeheartedly.

I will try to keep you informed if any more dreams come or if anything else happens. Right now, I think I want to lay low. You said I could remain anonymous and I would like to take you up on that. The last thing I want is somebody at (REDACTED) to hear about this and then I would have to face not only people that I grew up with but family members. Thank you, J"

I apologize for the redaction of location information. There have been instances in the past when other so-called investigators (outside of our groups) have harassed witnesses and others. I swear to never let that happen again, regardless of what people may say.

'J' is a unique witness and experiencer. I believe that she may have had contact with otherworldly entities before and after this incident.

I will note that a remote view session was conducted with 3 other participants who had no knowledge of this incident. This included a monitor (myself), a control and two viewers. The results were much in line with what 'J' told me, including a description of the individual who confronted her at lunch. It was determined that the encounter took place on October 28, 2019. Other detailed information may be released after our team gets a better handle on this investigation.

JULY 3, 2019 – ROSEMONT, IL

ON NOVEMBER 18, 2019, Manuel Navarette received a report of an earlier sighting during the previous summer:

"I've been following your investigations into the Chicago Mothman for about a year and a half now. I've always been skeptical and always thought there was a logical explanation for them until I had a sighting myself. It was after reading the latest sightings in Rosemont that I decided to write in and report mine. I work for a company that services billboards along the expressway. We service both the static boards as well as the electronic ones that are popping up all over the place. I was working on a billboard that is alongside The Jane Addams

Tollway (I-90). It sits behind the MB Bank building in Rosemont just off Evenhouse Avenue.

I was working on replacing some lights that shine up onto the board and about to wrap it up and come down. As I was gathering some tools, I saw something out of the corner of my eye and turned to see a large black animal that was coming down toward the nearby Des Plaines River. At first, I thought it was a crow but then realized that this thing was way too big to be a crow. It was black, but the wings had a sort of sheen to them and were not as black as the rest of his body which was solid black. It flapped its wings faster as it descended and then disappeared behind the tree line on what looked like the opposite bank of the river. I did not see anything else after that. I came down off the board and put my tools away and left the area. I was a bit of a chicken and decided not to walk toward the trees to see if I could find or see something. BR"

Manuel spoke with the witness at length about the sighting. He stated that he had just finished replacing some lights on the billboard and was putting all his tools away when he saw the entity. According to the witness, the entity was flying north parallel to the Des Plaines River descended to the bank of the river next to St. Nicholas Ukrainian Catholic Cemetery. At first, the witness stated that he thought it was a crow but realized that it was not making any noise. He stated that he sees crows in and around the river all the time and they are always cawing and making a racket and that this object was not making any noise whatsoever. He estimated that it was about 6 feet tall but could not give a definitive answer as there were no points of reference to compare it to.

The witness said he watched it for a few seconds before he lost sight of it when it went below the tree line on what seems to be the opposite bank of the river. The witness said he came down from the billboard and started putting his tools back in the truck and left the area. When asked if he walked toward the area to investigate, he stated that he was too "chickenshit" to go find out and left without investigating.

After talking with the witness, he seemed very grounded and down to Earth and shows no signs of fabricating any of this story. When asked questions designed to divert the path or embellish the story, the witness stayed on course and stuck to the original description of his reported encounter. When asked why it took so long to report the sighting the witness stated that he initially forgot about the sighting until reading about the other more recent Rosemont sightings and that is what triggered him to report his sighting.

It was Manuel's opinion that the witness report is valid, and no initial indicators of hoaxing or fabrication exist. A field investigation of the area was required and was completed soon after.

NOVEMBER 26, 2019 – O'HARE INTERNATIONAL AIRPORT

MANUEL SOON RECEIVED a report of a sighting on the O'Hare International Airport property:

"I was at the airport picking up a load at Nippon (cargo area) at around 6:30 pm. I was already backed into a dock and was standing away from the truck smoking a cigarette while they loaded my truck. I was looking toward the runways, in the direction of the tunnel and that is when I noticed something that looked like a large bird standing just outside of the fence by the parking lot. It was not hard to miss because two street lamps were nearby. It looked like a person with wings that were stretched out and flapping. It was walking away from the

fence toward the open field and then began to flap its wings and disappeared."

Manuel spoke with the witness by telephone and was able to get a little more information regarding this sighting. The witness primarily speaks Spanish but was able to report this sighting with the help of his daughter and her boyfriend. The witness was standing away from his truck as it was being loaded, smoking a cigarette, when he said he caught movement out of the corner of his eye. He said that the being was standing near the parking lot and was illuminated by two streetlamps. The witness stated that the creature was about seven feet tall using the fence as a point of reference. When asked him how he was able to be so certain as to the height of this being, the driver stated he has been to this location multiple times and he estimates the fence to be about 8 feet high. When asked him how large the wings were, he said at least six feet across and black. He described the being as a 'demonio' (demon) or a 'duende' (goblin) and that it was solid black. The witness said he saw nothing that looked like eyes and he assumed the creature might have had his back turned to him. He stated that it walked with a gait, like a bird and that it was flapping its wings as it walked toward the large field that is by the runways and disappeared into the night.

The witness did state that when it disappeared, he quickly did the sign of the cross and asked the Virgin Mary for protection. He put out his cigarette and quickly walked back to his truck. When asked him why he did that, he stated that he felt a presence that was evil and was convinced that he had seen a demon. When asked to elaborate on this statement the witness refused to talk about it anymore for fear of it coming back. Manuel respected his wishes and went on to ask other questions about the time, conditions and if there were other potential witnesses to his sighting. He stated that there were others at the same facility, but many were either inside or in their trucks. When asked if he had seen something similar before, the witness stated that he had when he was a teenager back home in Mexico. The witness stated that he saw a solid black-winged creature that was circling an open field where he and other children were playing soccer. He stated it circled the field and made a loud screeching noise before flying off into the surrounding forest. When he asked him if he remembered the date of the sighting, he stated that he did not remember the exact date, but a week later there was a large earthquake in Mexico City. (For the record, the magnitude 8.0 earthquake that hit Mexico City was on September 19, 1985)

The witness seemed sincere, though scared that he had seen something demonic and evil. It is Manuel's opinion that the witness is telling the truth. Manuel conducted a field observation soon afterwards.

DECEMBER 6, 2019 – O'HARE INTERNATIONAL AIRPORT

On Saturday, December 7, 2019, I was alerted to a new and credible winged humanoid sighting at O'Hare International Airport. I personally talked to the witness 'DR' who, in turn, later talked to Tobias Wayland. DR provided the following information:

At approximately 10:20 pm local time on Friday, December 6, 2019, the witness DR had left work at a cargo facility at O'Hare International Airport in Rosemont, Illinois. DR turned left from Patton Dr. onto W. Higgins Rd. After travel west for approximately six hundred feet he noticed a tall dark entity with wings standing by the fence to his left. According to DR, the entity was one hundred feet or so from him. DR noticed the strikingly red glowing eyes of this winged humanoid. He stated that he later found the previously reported incident (on Phantoms & Monsters) near the O'Hare International cargo area and likened his sighting to be the same entity. But this time, the red eyes were observed.

DR said that he was shocked at the time and felt an overwhelming sense of dread rush over him. The witness is very credible and lucid. He promises to offer any follow-up or other witness information if it should surface. By this time, this was the seventh reported sighting in the Rosemont / O'Hare International area during the previous two months.

DECEMBER 3, 2019 – O'HARE INTERNATIONAL AIRPORT

THE FOLLOWING information was received by Manuel Navarette very soon after the previous report:

"My name is (REDACTED) and I live in (REDACTED), Illinois. I'm reluctantly writing to you to report something that I saw a week ago on Tuesday. A little background information first, I am (REDACTED) years old and I have worked at O'Hare since (REDACTED). Part of my job is to routinely patrol the fence lines that surround O'Hare international Airport. I will sometimes have a partner with me, mostly new hires who are going through initial training.

On the night of Tuesday, December 3, 2019, I was heading toward one of the airport cargo hubs. There are multiple hubs scattered throughout the airport. The hub was located on Express Center Drive and it houses at least 6 cargo companies. I was approaching the creek headed toward Montrose Ave when I saw this large person standing down in the creek bed. I stopped, thinking it was maybe a trucker who decided to wander down there to relieve himself.

I put on my lights and stopped my vehicle and was preparing to get out when this man turned toward me, and I saw two very bright red eyes. This thing appeared to be looking straight at me and then it turned and walked away. As it did it unfurled a set of wings and it began to flap them. It looked like a large goose when it wants to take off into the air. It took off into the air and was gone into the darkness. I was left there wondering what in the Hell had just happened and what I had just seen. After I got home, I spent the next few days looking for similar sightings and that is where I came across your website.

I'm going to be blunt here, I don't believe in hobgoblins and little green men. I'm sure that there must be a rational explanation for this. I have a reputation for being grounded and level-headed. I have worked too hard to get where I am and to have that all trashed by saying that I saw a red-eyed flying man, yet that is what I saw. I am torn between reporting this and keeping my mouth shut to protect my retirement. If I do report this, I want everything to be done to protect my identity."

Manuel contacted witness by telephone. The witness was extremely hesitant to speak and expressed a reluctance to proceed any further. But after confidentiality assurances were explained he was persuaded to speak with Manuel. The witness states that he has worked at O'Hare since 2003 and that he has never seen anything like what he witnessed on December 3, 2019. The witness describes the area, 'as heavily trafficked.'

This was verified by Manuel during a subsequent field investigation of the area. The area where the sighting occurred is one of the cargo hubs located around the perimeter of O'Hare and is active 24 hours a day. During the field investigation, multiple semi-trucks were seen leaving and arriving at the various warehouses in the hub.

The witness says he saw what looked like a man standing down by the creek and believed it was a person trying to relieve themselves and was going to stop and tell them to stop. This is when the witness says he saw two bright red eyes appear as the creature turned its head. He stated that it appeared as if it was looking at him. He then stated that the entity began to walk away from him, unfurled what appeared to be a pair of wings and was gone out of sight within a matter of seconds.

The witness concluded that when it turned and began to move away from him, it looked comparable to how a large goose would move and then take flight. When asked follow-up questions, the witness again became very hesitant to answer any more questions and said he did not want to do or say anything that would put his retirement into jeopardy. When asked if he reported the sighting to his superiors, the witness became agitated and said he was not looking to commit 'career suicide.' No further questions were asked as the witness was upset, and Manuel did not want the witness to become concerned any further than he already had.

MORE HIGH STRANGENESS AT O'HARE INTERNATIONAL AIRPORT

In mid-January 2020 I began to become aware of rumblings within the management of O'Hare International. It was obvious that they had been cognizant of the reports of winged humanoids generated by employees. After we received the report by the TSA security employee in December, I was confident the incident would become general knowledge at the airport.

A few reliable sources relayed to me that employees were being told by their supervisors not to mention any further sightings or encounters. Nonetheless, truck drivers and other personal may eventually contact us.

There was one report that was forwarded to me by Manuel Navarette that may have some connection to other incidents. On January 23, 2020, at around 1 am, a night shift worker at one of the cargo warehouses witnessed an egg-shaped craft:

"I was outside taking a smoke break and was on the phone with my girlfriend when I saw this thing pass over me. It was completely silent, but it was also extremely bright. As it passed over shafts of light were coming from this thing and projecting to the ground. It was moving very, very fast and then stopped right above that old cemetery that sits inside the airport. Then a brilliant blue light come from this thing toward the ground.

It was then that I saw something rise toward the object and it disappeared after about five seconds. It looked like it was a person, but I was standing too far away to get a good look at it. I can tell you that it looked a lot like a person getting sucked up into this thing. This object then rotated in place and within 3 seconds, this thing flew up toward the north and was gone within a second. I'm telling you it was the strangest thing I have ever seen in my entire life!

I stood there looking as it fade out and stayed out there for a few minutes before coming back to my senses and going back inside. This thing looked like it was over by the cemetery. If you want to, I will show you where it is. A lot of people don't even know this place is out there.

*This is not the first time I have ever seen things in the sky,
and I know that a lot of the people I work with here during the
night shift have seen lots of strange things here at this airport.
It seems to attract a lot of weird things."*

Manuel spoke with the witness by telephone and he
explained that he worked the night shift and during downtime,
he would walk outside to take a smoke break. It was during one
of these smoke breaks as he was talking on his phone that he first
noticed the lights from the object that he claimed flew overhead.
He claimed the object was egg-shaped and he estimated that the
object was about forty feet in diameter and about ten to twelve
feet high. The witness claimed the object was silent and was
shooting rays of light toward the ground. He says he watched as
it flew overhead and stopped above the Resthaven Cemetery.

The witness then said he watched as the object hovered
silently about twenty feet above the treetops for about 20
seconds before a brilliant blue light shot down from the object
and hit the ground below. The witness then stated that he saw
what looked like a person being lifted off the ground and into
the object. The witness states that he could not definitively see
what it was that was being lifted but that it looked a lot like a
humanoid shape. The witness stated he was too far away to
make a positive identification and he was too scared to approach
the object and get a closer look.

The witness went on to tell how the humanoid disappeared
in the brilliance of the light and that within a second or two, the
light ceased, and the object began to rotate in place in a clockwise motion. The object then shot off in a northerly direction
and was out of sight within a few seconds. The witness stated
that he walked back into the building, not wanting to be outside
anymore. The witness stated that he did not venture outside
again until the sun had begun to rise. The witness stated that

many of his colleagues have seen many strange things during the overnight hours around the facility where he works including strange orbs, lights in the sky not associated with airport activities. When asked if he had seen or had heard about any flying humanoid sightings, he advised he had not.

5

MORE FLYING HUMANOID INCIDENTS

OCTOBER 27, 1969 – ROLLING PRAIRIE, IN

I received a telephone call describing a harrowing account from the eyewitness Floyd R. Hancock. The incident occurred on the night of October 27, 1969, in Rolling Prairie, Indiana. Floyd was a young child at the time.

Floyd states that he and his family (mother, father, sister and grandmother) where living in a trailer situated on their family's land. The trailer had sustained damage on the roof, leaving a large hole. The hole was covered with a wide waterproof tarp until it was to be repaired.

Floyd and his baby sister shared a bedroom. He was awakened by a strange noise and a strong disagreeable odor. As he looked towards his sister's crib, he saw a tall winged humanoid staring down at her. The being slowing turned and looked at a horrified Floyd.

The description was a very tall being that was crouched a bit. He estimates that it stood seven to eight foot in height. The body and face had black hair. The leather-like wings were huge and shaped like that of a bat or gargoyle. It had muscular detached arms and legs. The body and face were thin and looked like a human skeleton with obvious sharp teeth. The eyes were dark. It also made a low garbled sound.

Floyd screamed in order to alert his parents in the adjoining room, but they never responded. His grandmother was alerted and came to his aid, though she was stunned at the sight and immediately fell to her knees.

The creature picked Floyd up into its arms and walked towards the living room, where it ascended through the hole in the ceiling. It's obvious it had moved the tarp in order to gain access inside the trailer. Floyd remembers being very cold and wet, and hearing his grandmother screaming as the winged humanoid took off into the sky. He has no idea how long he was gone, but only remembers waking in his bed among his panicked parents and grandmother.

Floyd states that his grandmother witnessed the entire event and documented it. His living relatives concur with the account, since his grandmother recalled what had happened to each of them. His grandmother passed away in 1985.

Floyd's parent woke after the abduction. It seems that they were somehow placed into a hypnotic state until the winged being left the premises with Floyd. After several minutes, they all heard scratching noises and a loud thud on the roof. Floyd's father immediately gained access to the roof where he saw his son lying unconscious. They were able to quickly bring Floyd into the trailer, dry him off and place him in his bed. They were reluctant to call the authorities or seek medical assistance because of the bizarre event.

Floyd recovered but has endured emotional problems his entire life which he attributes to the abduction. At the time of 'The Mothman Prophecies' film release, he had a mental breakdown after watching it in a theater. He literally had to leave during the scene where the Mothman caused the automobile crash and death. He has not attempted to watch the film since then.

I asked Floyd why he called me. He stated that he had received a call from his cousin who was aware of the winged humanoid sightings in Indiana. That's when he was given my contact information.

Floyd included the sketch. He was very forthright, but quite nervous, and seemed relieved that there had been other eyewitnesses to a similar winged being.

OCTOBER 30, 2019 – PARK RIDGE, IL

I RECEIVED the following email on Thursday October 31, 2019:

> "I was driving home north on Talcott Rd. at about 9:30 pm on the evening of Wednesday, October 30th. As I was

approaching the intersection with Boardwalk Place, I saw something walk across the road. At first, I thought it was a deer as we get them every now and again. That changed when this thing stopped in the middle of the road and faced me head-on. I panicked and came to a stop. That is when this thing spread out with what looked like enormous wings and screeched at me before bounding towards the woods. This thing looked like a seven-foot man, thin and with two very large red eyes that were illuminated. My headlights were on this thing and it was solid black. It looked like it had skin and not feathers. The wings looked like they were attached to its back. I was scared half out of my wits and there was no way in Hell I was going to get out of my car and go after it into the woods. I slammed my foot on the accelerator and took off for home where I told my husband about it. It was his idea that I report this to you. LA"

The witness 'LA' responded to my request for an interview:

"Hello Lon,

I would rather not talk to anyone. I would rather correspond via email as to protect myself. It's nothing against you, but I don't want my kids to find out and have them think I'm seeing things.

I hope you understand. LA"

I have good reason to believe that what was stated in the email is true. I received a bit more information from the witness, and I conducted some research on the witness' identification which checked out. The encounter and description in the account was never changed. Hopefully, LA or others will eventually come forward with further details.

FALL 2011 – DOWNERS GROVE, IL

I RECEIVED the following email from a witness on December 6, 2019:

"Though I've spoke of my encounters at least a thousand times I've always attributed the sightings to a giant owl or bat of some kind. I realize today, that this creature was way too big to be any bird. In the Fall of 2011, my brother-in-law and I were sitting around a small bonfire in my backyard on a beautiful Indian summer night enjoying what was left of the nice weather. All of a sudden, my brother-in-law whispers, "Dude, check that out." I slowly turned to look toward the south where he seemed to be focused and asked what he was looking at. He said look at the big oak two houses down. I did as he started lining me up using a few landmarks and just then I noticed what he was looking at about twenty feet up in the tree. This huge creature seemed to kind of jump, maybe dead drop out intentionally. It fell forward spreading or opening what looked more like bat wings or a cape, then a set of wings. The wings never closed or even flapped before this thing disappeared behind the fence. In other words it glided from at least twenty feet up almost straight down until it disappeared behind the fence. There was no noise from the tree branches, not a crackle from the leaves it landed on nor a sound from anything. None at all, dead silence!

Needless to say, we were freaked out. We quickly went inside, trying to rationalize the whole thing. We decided we'd call it a big owl from then on. I've always thought it was something other than a bird. He and I will still occasionally joke about that night being the "Batman" experience.

My other encounter happened several miles from here. I was alone driving to my favorite spot on the Kankakee River southbound on I-55 crossing the Illinois River bridge at dawn. Something flew out from under that bridge right across my line of sight completely covering my windshield, blocking my forward sight for a second. Then it was gone. In that case all I know is that thing was also huge and seemed to be brown in the new morning light. Mike"

I called and talked to the witness. I also received verification about the incident from the brother-in-law. The size was estimated to be six feet in height and definitely humanoid, with legs and attached arms to the bat-like wings. Black in color with a wing span of ten feet or so. Lights from the street and neighbor's house helped to illuminate the being, but they were unable to get specific details of the face. The time was estimated to be before midnight.

AUGUST 2017 – KENOSHA, WI

I RECEIVED a witness email on December 10, 2019:

"Hello, thank you for putting the article of the Man-Bat online. A couple of years (August 2017) ago a friend and I where in Kenosha, Wisconsin on our way to northern Illinois (where we lived at the time) after getting tattoos. It was somewhere between 2 and 3 am. I remember before approaching the train tracks on a road near downtown, my friend and I noticed a man-like creature with wings cross the street slow enough for us to be able to see the shape and figure of what it was. But in an instant it was gone as if it was never there to begin with. During the four hour drive back home we discussed the thing that we had seen. Keep in mind we both had seen it regardless if it was the late night or the lack of

sleep. We still can't explain the fact that we both saw the same thing. I have been curious to the possibility of a creature or humanoid-like being existing. But now after reading the article and moving from Illinois to northwest Indiana, I am even more interested now then ever. Thank you." JV

It was later determined that the location was a public railway line that ended at 52nd St. near 13th Ave. There was a railway overpass there as well. These tracks by the road stopped at 52nd St. The being was seen crossing the road at this location. The description was very similar to others we have received, about five to six feet in height, dark colored with bat-like wings.

There was another sighting report (around the same time - August 2017) of a similar being crossing a road just south of Kenosha on Rt. 32 near the Illinois / Wisconsin border. Very similar description. Witness was fearful of talking about the incident in greater detail.

LATE OCTOBER 2019 – HOFFMAN ESTATES, IL

I RECEIVED another email from a witness on December 12, 2019:

"Hello, I am writing to you today in regards to the Mothman/Human Owl. This is DG and JG. We live at The Reserve in Hoffman Estates in Illinois and our apartment complex is next to an empty cornfield and across from Barrington, Illinois there is a forest preserve. My husband and I live on the third floor of the complex as we face another building, but can also see towards the cornfield to our right. We also have lots of trees around our building almost as tall as the building itself.

We would normally go out to our porch every night to smoke a cigarette, and about a month and two weeks ago (late October 2019), we went out at about 9-10 pm. We usually leave our phones inside so we can enjoy some chat and gaze upon at the stars, or even see a pack of coyotes roaming around the streets and apartments, or sometimes even heading back into the field towards the forest (keep in mind this field has no crop so it is empty and you can see towards the street). Well, that specific night my husband was to my right and he is taller than me. So I was talking to him while taking a puff, when I noticed something in the pine tree behind him. Right at the top of the tree, not in between the branches, right at the top. He noticed I wasn't paying attention so he turned around to look, and sure enough there was what we thought was a huge owl looking out towards the field then looking back around. So after several seconds, maybe thirty seconds, we started to question each other, "what is that?" "Is that an owl?" This thing was pitch black but its wings and shape were huge, as you can see the dark silhouette in front of the sky which was lighter.

I recall continuing to smoke as we tried to examine this creature looking around. Once we had noticed it, I don't recall 'it' ever looking at us. We were already a few minutes outside before I noticed it, so I'm not sure if it ever looked down at us. I was more focused on the body shape though. I could see huge, long black wings. We couldn't really see any details as it was super dark. My husband was trying to get closer to the edge to get a good look at it but we could really just see the long wings and huge shape.

Well, after a while, we said, "yeah, it might just be an owl, a pretty big one for sure." We came inside our complex which is the roof of the building. Normally at night we could hear the animals climbing on the rails and roof, but our roommate, whose room is next to the porch, states he always hears something walking at night by his window or above it. I'm not sure if it's that creature. The tree is right next to us so it could easily climb onto the building.

We thought nothing of it until we read the article about a semi-truck driver who spotted something similar at O'Hare Airport, which is not far from here. Once we saw that we just stared at each other because we recall what we saw. We sometimes step out for a moment to see if we find it again but so far it hasn't returned.

Feel free to email me back with any questions. Thank you. DG"

I contacted the witnesses by telephone. There is not much more information to add, though I truly believe they both observed something remarkable.

NOVEMBER 1, 2015 – CHICAGO, IL

I RECEIVED the following account on December 19, 2019:

"Hello, a friend shared an NPR article about the Mothman sightings in Chicago and I was shocked when I came upon your website and research.

On November 1, 2015 around 10 am I was chatting on the phone with a good friend, minding my business making plans for brunch, when I glanced out my bedroom window and immediately noticed something out of place. A very large "crow man" hovering over a high-rise apartment building about a block away from my house. A man, jet black from head to toe, upright hovering in the air about five feet above the Midway Plaisance Senior Apartments on E. 60th Street. For reference, this is a 17-story high-rise apartment building directly across the street from Washington Park on the southside of Chicago (miles from downtown and not a lot of high-rises in the area).

So I'm on the phone with my friend but I go silent as I'm watching this thing hovering and kind of spinning around slowly over the building and my friend on the phone starts asking me if I'm still there. I start describing to her what I'm looking at and of course she thinks I'm crazy. By the time I get off the phone to try and take a picture the thing starts to float away and move westbound behind some trees where I lost sight of it. I call my friend back and she is trying to rationalize that I saw some sort of life-sized leftover Halloween decoration flying twenty stories in the air like a balloon. I can't say exactly what I saw as it was unlike anything I have ever seen or could even imagine, but it was alive and wasn't any damn balloon. The whole sighting only lasted about 60 seconds but I got a good look at it from my 3rd floor window before it "flew" away.

The thing had wings tucked behind it, but didn't need them to hover or move around. I wouldn't say it "flew" at all, it literally hovered in a standing position. It was jet black from head to toe, front to back. It had to be about eight feet tall, and I could clearly make out a head, arms, legs, and wings folded behind it. There wasn't a single cloud in the sky, and the sky was a crisp bright blue. It was so sunny that its jet black body looked iridescent with shades of blue and purple reflecting off of it in the sunlight as it did a slow 360 degree turn. From the iridescent color and wings I can best describe this thing as a "crow man." It almost looked like how the feathers of a crow looks iridescent from where I was standing. At the time I googled "crow man sightings in Chicago" and couldn't find any other sightings on the internet to justify what I saw, or *help anyone believe me. I only told about three to four close friends and family members and they just kind of joked, filed it away mentally, and we all moved on.*

Well, fast forward to about a week ago and one of the friends I had told my sighting to sends me this NPR article where I came across your collection of other reported sightings, each sounding eerily similar to what I saw. Now, I'm a busy college educated 'mom-preneur' raising two little ones, with a demanding career, and a side business, and don't have time for any visits from the Men in Black, the government, or a creepy Mothman seeking revenge for snitching on him. But how is this not national news or a public safety alert? I literally started crying when I clicked on the map in that article and read a reported sighting from Washington Park in 2011 just a few hundred feet away from the high-rise building where I saw it in 2015. For reference, Washington Park is 372 acres, and this particular area is pretty close to the large pond on the southeast side of the park by 60th and Cottage Grove.

Wish I had more to share but honestly I was too terrified to run outside after this thing to take a picture. It had wings and didn't need them to fly. I wish I could go back to minding my business, but really hope you can expose what is going on here. Let me know if you have any questions. M"

The witness and I emailed back and forth, though she fairly well summed up the sighting in her initial report. The 'hovering' aspect of the 'crow man' closely match other sightings in 2017 throughout Chicago and the surrounding area. Very intriguing account.

JANUARY 1, 2000 & OCTOBER 2002 – ROCKFORD, IL

On December 24, 2019, I talked to a witness 'JL' who had a UFO experience and, then later, a winged humanoid encounter near the same location.

On the evening of January 1, 2000, JL and her son were traveling on Spring Creek Rd in Rockford, Illinois. As they approached Rock Creek they both observed a large diamond-shaped craft hovering above the creek. The craft was brightly lit and there was a distinct beam of light coming from the bottom towards the creek. JL slowed the car and the craft suddenly cut off the beam. At the same time, the craft slowly ascended into the night sky.

JL and her son had lingering dreams after the incident and both started to notice paranormal activity around them.

Then on an October night in 2002, at around 8 pm, JL was again driving on Spring Creek Rd near Rock Creek. She observed a large winged figure approaching her head-on. By the time this flying anomaly got near her, it swooped up and over the car. JL states that the winged being was humanoid in shape with two leg-like structures trailing below it. The wing span was so wide that it literally blocked out all the street lights. She estimates that it was six feet in height, black in color and had large wings approximately twelve feet in total width.

She immediately stopped the car, got out and looked down the road behind her. The winged being had vanished, but she noticed that the trees were moving as if a huge gust of wind had gone through them. She also stated that the being never flapped its wings. It seemed to be propelled by an unknown force.

JL has experienced a sense of consternation and anxiety ever since the incident, even though she now lives Tennessee.

LATE SUMMER 2001 – BERWYN, IL

TOBIAS WAYLAND of the Singular Fortean Society received and published the following account:

"In 2001 we were in my backyard in Berwyn, which is next to Cicero, just outside of Chicago. We were having a picnic in the backyard. It was about nine or ten o'clock at night. Now, it scares me to talk about this, because I don't want to bring bad juju on myself," she said over the phone. "I was in the backyard cleaning up and I look up in the air—it was a beautiful, moonlit night, just a couple days before 9/11—and the moon's out but it's kind of cloudy, I've got tiki torches in the backyard and those really big balls that light up like half a block. I'm by myself, outside, cleaning and gathering stuff off of the table, and I see four humongous—they looked humongous— people, they looked like men, and they were all black and they had big wings, I mean HUGE wings. The wings were not feathery, they were bat wings or demon wings. I looked at them and there were four in a row, and they looked like they were standing up [horizontally] as they flew. They were muscular, they were big, and I looked up and went 'Oh my God, what the [expletive] is that?'"

The witness offered that she's "sensitive," in the sense of having a natural affinity for psychic phenomena.

"I've got these weird gifts and they've always been scary to me; I never understood them," she said. "I found out after years of therapy and talking to priests that I'm blessed, and you can either learn to use it or suppress it. I chose to suppress it, because it's scary."

That sensitivity might help explain what came next.

"They didn't hear me, they were too high up to hear me, but two of them looked directly at me, and when they looked at me, they had red eyes," she said. "I freaked out, because they looked directly into my eyes. I ran into my house, and I was starting to cry because I was freaking out. My cousin, who has since passed away, said, 'What's wrong? What happened? What's the matter?' But I was too afraid to speak; I just wanted to go back outside to make sure they were gone. I went out there and they were gone. They never came back. I was afraid for weeks after that to go outside."

Like many witnesses, she shared her experience with a few people, only to be mocked. Still, she stands by her story.

"This was not my imagination. I don't do drugs and I don't drink. This blew my mind; completely blew my mind. I told some people at work, but of course they laughed at me. They taunted me; thought I was crazy. To this day, I know what I saw. I won't let anyone try to manipulate my story or tell me I was hallucinating," she said.

Several years ago, over a decade after the sighting, one of her sons mentioned to her the significance of the date and its proximity to the national tragedy of 9/11.

The witness' testimony and corresponding weather data tentatively indicate the night of the sighting to be September 8, three days before the terrorist attacks.

"My son, who's 32, said to me 'Mom, this is really odd, but did you ever think that 9/11 happened right after you saw [those winged creatures]?' I said, 'No, I never thought of that.' He said, 'You saw four of them, right?' I said, 'Yeah.' He said, 'Right in front of each other like perfectly aligned, and they

were huge with humongous wings. They were out to do something; you could tell they were on a mission. You got the [Twin Towers of the World Trade Center], you've got [the Pentagon], and you've got [Flight 93] that crashed in a field.' I said, 'Oh my God, I never thought of that. I never ever thought of that,'" she said of the possible correspondences.

Many believe that sightings of 'Mothman,' as red-eyed, winged creatures are often called, are portents of tragedy, although this belief is contested within the paranormal community.

Regardless of the veracity of that connection, the effect this experience had on the witness is undeniable.

"I never even knew Mothman existed, never heard any of the stories," she said, *"There's a lot of stuff that I never dabbled in, ever. Which is scary, because you've got nobody to talk to, and you're afraid to talk to people. You're afraid to say what you've seen. I never called the police; I was so scared."*

Did the sighting of four red-eyed winged humanoids in Berwyn, IL foretell the tragic events of 9/11? I suppose we should maintain an open mind to the possibility.

SUMMER 2016 NEAR CHESTERLAND, OH

My colleague Jamie Brian notified me of apparent incident with a winged cryptid near Chesterland, Ohio. The original report was as follows:

"I'm 32 years old and had never seen anything supernatural or alien in my life until last summer. I had always been and still

am very much a skeptic, and to this day I try to convince myself that what I saw was actually a really big hawk or something. But I know I'm lying to myself.

It was around 3:45 am, I'm driving west on Rt. 322 towards Chesterland, Ohio. I'm driving a Freightliner box truck with a load of newspapers. In the summer time at night, there's always a layer of fog hanging down around the ground, and the moon was bright and the stars were out. Going about 50 mph through the hills I see this dark figure in the moonlight that was coming right at me. It looked HUGE so I slammed the brakes and actually ducked down instinctively because I was driving right towards it at windshield level. I heard a big THUD as the figure had gone over the cab and smacked right into the flat aluminum box right behind the cab at probably 40 mph. I kept my foot on the brake and came to a stop on the side of the road probably about seventy-five yards from where the impact happened. Wondering if it had smashed in the top of the box and thinking maybe I could see what it was I hit, I got out and looked around. The box wasn't smashed in so I walked around to the back of the truck and that's when I saw it in the moonlight almost as clear as day.

This thing was huge. I thought for sure it was dead, but all of a sudden it rolled over and that's when I saw it's "bat-like" wings, not bird shaped. It rolled over and stood up on two legs and was at least six feet tall. The thing looked right at me with its red/orange eyes and I was literally frozen in fear. I could not move at all. Then it spread its huge wings out, jumped up and flew off. I ran back to the truck and took off towards Chesterland as fast as I could and spent the rest of the night on edge and trying to rationalize what I had just saw. The closest thing I could describe it to the 'Jeepers Creepers' monster, but I wasn't that close to it that I could see facial features and much detail. Just the six foot tall bat-winged man with orange-red eyes. I do that route for work every week and every time I go through that stretch on Rt. 322 I get uneasy. It freaks me out almost six months later." RW

I reached out to the eyewitness and received more information:

"The truck wasn't damaged, but when I got to the gas station in Chesterland, you could see that something huge had just hit the box because there was like an imprint in all the dirt and dead bugs and griminess that collects on the front of the box. I wanted to try and crawl up on top of the cab to get a better look and possibly see if there was any sort of blood or hair or anything that would possibly show evidence of whatever it was but I would have needed a ladder and someone helping me. I looked it over with a flashlight really well but didn't see anything other than the imprint.

As far as the creature itself, basically the thing that stood out to me the most were its eyes. I'll never forget how much they mesmerized me with that fiery orange color. It was almost like it could see into my soul. It only lasted for a couple seconds before it jumped up and flew off, but I did feel some sort of connection with it. I was very much afraid of it though. I'm just about to leave for the same route I was on that night when it happened. I still remember exactly where it happened. When I go through there tonight I'll try to find the closest cross roads or something that I can pinpoint exactly where it was on a map." RW

SUMMER 1999 NEAR JOPLIN, MO

On December 19, 2017, I was contacted by 'Edward' in Kansas City, Kansas by telephone, after he read a post that referenced my recently published book.

Edward wanted to relay an encounter that he and his cousin had in the summer of 1999 between 10-11 pm local time. They were traveling southbound on I-49 towards Joplin, Missouri (Edward was driving). He could not recall the exact area, but they were not too many miles from Joplin.

He states that he noticed a tall figure quickly running from the direction of medium to his left, then directly in front of his car. Both he and his cousin observed this human-like being, that they immediately said to each other that it 'looked like a gargoyle.' The headlights illuminated the humanoid so well that both witnesses were able to get a good description of it. The 'gargoyle' was at least six and a half feet in height and had dark leathery hairless skin all over its body. The being looked towards the witnesses, and the face had stark flatten facial features with large deep set eyes. There were large wings that laid flat on its back, but were extended as it reached the other (right) side of the highway. Edward believes the being had begun to ascend into the air, and above the field.

Edward noted that he had no other comparison for the humanoid, other than that of 'gargoyle.' But after he watched the movie 'Jeepers Creepers' after the film's release in 2001, he stated that the humanoid was 'very similar' to the 'Creeper' character. Both witnesses kept quiet about the encounter, until a few years later when Edward married his wife. He and his cousin both recounted the incident to her.

The witness seemed grateful that he could 'tell his story without someone thinking he was crazy.'

JANUARY 2011 – CHIPPEWA FALLS, WI

"Hello, I recently listened to a podcast on 'The Higher Side Chats,' and got this website from that. I have never known where to report this incident so I have just kept it to myself. However, I would like to add my encounter/experience to the inventory of this mystery.

Everything that has been described in the Chicago accounts of a bat-like creature, is pretty identical to what I saw with a few exceptions. My sighting took place in Chippewa Falls, WI in January 2011. It was between 9:00 pm and 11:00 pm when I saw it. I was outside smoking a cigarette, and I saw a human-sized being with bat-like wings fly over head. It flew/glided a little higher than the street lights. The wings were somewhat transparent, exactly how a bat looks, except that it did not flap its wings. It glided past. My reaction was not negative, nor positive, just speculative. I was in a moment of 'what was that?' I would also like to note that I did not see any red eyes.

I would also like to add another sighting (not mine however, this is a sighting from my boyfriend's friend). It was in Fort Atkinson, WI area. Around January 2014 at 3:00 am He said it was big and it was standing by the river (Rock River). He refused to look at it because it freaked him out so bad.

In conclusion, I think there is some connection with water. Chippewa Falls is known for its water source. Rock River is a major river, and now Lake Michigan. Please feel free to contact me if you have any further questions regarding the sighting. Sincerely, SB"

I CONTACTED the witness and asked if they would provide more details:

"It was the size of a full-grown human. I just remember the wings being big and a little translucent (just like a bat). Actually it kind of reminded me of 'Jeepers Creepers.' But bats aren't around in winter and they are small and flap their wings constantly and fast. This was huge and glided. The place were I physically witnessed this event [my dad's driveway] has had strange things happen from time to time. But that was the only time I saw that creature thing. No one else was there to see it. Many years ago there were accidents by the intersection where I saw it. I was told that people died there. But I cannot verify that part as fact. SB"

October 2017 near Ocala, FL

On November 24, 2017, I received a telephone call from a woman who described a bizarre encounter while traveling with a friend on Rt. 40 near Ocala, Florida. The witness was in the front passenger seat, as they were returning to Ocala after spending the day in Dunnellon. It was approximately 3 pm on an unknown day in mid-October 2017. She observed a human-like being 'gliding' slowly above the treetops near the road. She watched this strange sight for several seconds as they approached and passed the anomaly. She commented to the driver, who also saw the unknown being.

The witness described the being as gliding horizontally just above the trees. It was shaped like a human, but had no wings or device keeping it aloft. It was wrapped in a black material or membrane. The face was that of a man, but very pale with jet black hair on its head. She states that it was about five feet in length and that she got as close as thirty feet. to the being. So she was quite close and able to obtain a good description. She also said that she was very shocked by the encounter and that the sighting has bothered her since.

Ocala is located in Marion County, and just west of the Ocala National Forest and east of Goethe State Park. Both of these forests are well-known for a large number of anomalies, including Skunk Apes, UFOs, cryptid canines, strange humanoids and unexplained spiritual activity. There have also been many weird natural occurrences as well. I have received a fair amount of reports from the Ocala National Forest region in the past.

NOVEMBER 2016 NEAR WEST ALTON, MO

On May 29, 2018, I received an email in reference to an encounter along the Mississippi River:

"Hello Mr. Strickler - in mid-November 2016, my son and I had been duck hunting from a blind in the Upper Mississippi Waterfowl Area, not far from West Alton, Missouri. It was about 5:15 pm and we were walking back to my truck. I had parked in a small lot off of Harbor Point Rd. and we had to walk about five hundred yards.

As we walked along the road, my son noticed a huge black thing descending towards the water's edge. I had never seen anything that large flying anywhere. It definitely wasn't a Bald Eagle or a crane, and as it got closer to the ground we were both shocked that it looked like a human!

It wasn't flapping its wings, but was gliding on a slow downward angle. It was about fifty yards from us, but there was enough light that we could clearly see it. The wings were outstretched and were very wide. The wing shape was similar to that of a bat, but huge! The color was dark, almost black.

The body was tapered like a well-built man with long legs. The head was small compared to the body, so I definitely knew it was not human. We were both caught off-guard and were mesmerized by what we were seeing. It landed in the thick weeds by the water and was obscured from our sight.

At that point, we both wanted to get out of there because we had no idea what this thing was. As we quickly walked along the road, we saw this thing crawling out of the weeds and into a small clearing. It was literally pushing itself forward on the ground with its legs and wings in the direction of the water. We could hear the sound it was making as it 'crawled' on the damp ground and mud. It didn't look like it was struggling, but it was an awkward way to move around. Though it had legs, I could not make out its feet. I assumed this was the way it actually moved on the ground. It slide into the water, then raised up a few times; like a swimmer doing a breast stroke. Then it disappeared into the murky water.

My son will not go to that location anymore, but I'd really like to know what we saw. I told a co-worker, who is also a duck hunter, about the incident. He seemed interested at the time, but I'm sure he doesn't believe me. I've never heard of anything similar to this thing, either around here or anywhere else. Do you have any idea of what this was? I saw your Google ad for humanoid sightings, so I looked you up. We can talk if you'd like. Thanks." JK

I able to talk by telephone to 'JK' a few days after receiving the email. I asked the witness why he waited so long to contact anyone. He said that it took him a while to actually believe what he and his son had seen was real. He described the wing span as twelve to fifteen feet with very wide bat-like wings. He also said that the head was small and kind of shaped like a football with a slight point on the top. He did not see detached arms, but by the way it moved along the ground, the arms were most likely part of the wings. It made no sounds other than those made while it crawled. I also asked if they had a cell phone with them and why they hadn't taken photos. JK said he didn't even realize that until they got back to the car. His son refused to discuss the incident.

It's an interesting encounter and comparable to the information I gathered from an individual in northwest Indiana, who told me that he and his wife had been observing this being feeding in the water. I am curious as to its characteristics underwater. Is it an amphibian or are there gills somewhere on the body? Then again, it may be something totally unknown. Just another question we are left with.

SEPTEMBER 16, 2017 – COACHELLA, CA

I RECEIVED A WRITTEN account of a sighting from a witness in California:

"On September 16, 2017, early morning about 5:15 am in Coachella, CA. near 4th and Palm Ave. I observed an unknown winged creature, bigger than any kind of bird I have ever seen. I've seen condors in the past, but this was much bigger. It was all black with a huge wing span that was at least ten feet; possible larger. It was at an altitude of one hundred to one hundred and fifty feet and gliding over my location towards the southeast. The wings had an outline of a bat's wing. It looked very much human, almost 'demonic' I felt; bony arms hanging down with claw-like hands and long legs extended behind. The body had to have been seven feet or more in length. It was making no noise, but I felt like it knew I was looking at it and I was fearful at what I was seeing. I told my

spouse and he said it must have been a large bat. I looked up bats, flying fox and the like, and this did not match the description.

We have seen lots of drones, and those are quick, large and have an aerodynamic body. This creature looked nothing like a drone or any other bird that we can identify. I contacted you after searching again on Google, and in relation to the Chicago winged humanoids.

Have there been any other similar sightings in the valley or in California? Thank you." KE

I contacted the witness by telephone. She says that she reported this sighting to the UFO reporting agencies and a cryptid investigator, but never heard back from anyone. This is the first related sighting that I have received from southern California. The witness comes from an USAF family and is well aware of aerial objects.

SUMMER 2011 NEAR MOOSE LAKE, MN

I RECEIVED a telephone call from an eyewitness 'DH' who encountered a winged humanoid while driving:

DH had recently come across the Chicago area winged humanoid posts and subsequent reports I had received in 2017-18. This was the first time DH had been aware of these sightings. This is why DH contacted me directly, in order to report his experience from 2011.

DH and a companion were driving south on I-35, after leaving the Black Bear Casino and on their way back to Moose Lake, Minnesota. It was a clear moonlit night, approximately 2 am. DW was driving a sports car.

As he was driving, he observed a large winged being quickly descending from the sky in front of them. They first saw it drop straight down with wings horizontal and open. It was at least one mile away and what DH estimates at 2000-3000 foot altitude. It literally looked like a human with wide bat-like wings, that spanned across both freeway lanes. The being glided towards the car, as if it was going to collide with the windshield. In fact, DH's companion coiled expecting an impact. DH braced himself for a collision, but suddenly the winged being flew over the vehicle. Both occupants were extremely shaken, to the point where DH pulled over onto the shoulder.

DH stated that the being was dark brown in color, with a shiny wet-like appearance. The wings were leather-like and quite large. The body was five to six feet in length and thin, with a narrow head that had pointed ears. The eyes were hollow and dark. The being never flapped or moved its wings, as if it had another means of propulsion.

DH never reported the encounter and felt that no one would ever believe him. He felt comfortable relaying the encounter to me after reading about the Chicago incidents.

DH provided the following update the day after the above post:

"We both noticed and saw what looked like a wide, somewhat glossy object drop straight down super fast like a spider would do when it drops on its vertical web line to lower its self. As it dropped and stopped suddenly just feet above the horizon as it then instantly proceeded to glide towards my low profile sports car at, what I estimate, about the same speed I was heading towards it. So we are heading towards each other now at about 140 MPH. I saw it in my high beams as it headed directly *towards my car's windshield. I waited till it appeared imminent it was going to collide with my windshield which was about twenty feet I guess. My view of the wings, face, shoulders were brief but amazing before I ducked sideways while trying to maintain control of my car. The lower part of my body just went numb and with lower torso goose bumps in a way I have never experienced. This creature defied physics as it dropped straight down, not an angled glide. It is as if the air went right through its wings and did appear to drop faster than gravity could pull any object down. Its bat-like wings nearly spanned the two freeway lanes. It made no sense to us then or now." DH*

The eyewitness is a well-known and respected professional in the entertainment industry. I truly believe that his report is consistent with other inquiries my associates and I have received concerning these winged humanoids.

JULY 2013 – CHERRY HILL, NJ

I RECEIVED an interesting report from New Jersey on July 22, 2015:

"I came across your site looking for answers of what my daughter and I saw in the sky and there are similar stories to ours. I am from Cherry Hill, NJ and approximately two years ago to this day my daughter and I were riding our bikes. It was bright that night due to a full moon. Not many clouds in the sky but a few that would once in a while make the night darker.

We stopped by a friend's house. Her and her two daughters came out and we where all just talking. I happened to look up in the sky and there's this flying long human shaped thing with a wing span approximately seven to eight feet wide. It reminded me of the movie 'Jeepers Creepers.' My mouth just kind of opened and I was speechless and pointing as it went behind the cloud near the moon. I told them what I had just witnessed. Everyone kind of giggled and I told them it did not come out of the cloud yet to keep looking. Well, to our eyes it appeared again. My daughter just stood there watching it repeating herself, 'Mom what is that?' I know she had that same hard-to-swallow feeling I did, while my friend's two girls ran inside screaming. We watched as it flapped and soared near the moon till it disappeared into the clouds again and never came out.

I know what I had seen that night, but wouldn't know what to call it except a flying human-like creature. An experience I would never take back and when I hear others, I really want to believe they had seen the same thing I had. My daughter to this day (now 14) feels there is so much out there we really don't know much about. What is myth and what is real? A night we will never forget and keeping herself busy researching the Jersey Devil to Mothman and Slender Man. It's out there!" - Strasse7

Because of the distance, the wingspan could have easily surpassed seven to eight feet. Very interesting and there were multiple witnesses to this sighting. Once again, a witness refers to the character in 'Jeepers Creepers.'

AUGUST 1990 IN NEWTON ABBOTT, DEVONSHIRE, UK

I RECEIVED the following account from UFO investigator Ken Pfeifer, which was forwarded to him by a colleague. We researched and investigated other activity in the area that may have been associated with this phenomenon:

"My adventure into the unknown began back in 1990. I remember it was very hot that year in Devon and the heat wave lasted for weeks. I think it was August. I'm not sure of the exact date but I do remember there being a hosepipe ban in Devon and other parts of the country. I remember the grass being dry just like straw.

I will never forget it. I was standing in the back garden of my old house when I just happened to look up and see something black far off in the distance. Whatever it was it appeared to be descending from the sky, gliding through the air at great speed. It was heading in my direction and I was having real trouble identifying what it could be. It was too large to be a bird and it looked like it was the size of a large man. I was very perplexed as it got closer. I thought that it was a skydiver. This is where my life changed forever.

The creature unfolded its large bat-like wings and began to flap them with tremendous force. I could hear a whooshing sound as the wings of the creature made contact with the air. I was holding a glass of Coca-Cola in my right hand and with shock I dropped it on the ground. I was so scared I did not know what to do. I just stood there gazing intently at the creature. Time seemed to slow down as it flew right over me casting a large black shadow on the ground around me.

I got a really good look at the creature. There was no visible head on its body and on its chest there were two large round glowing red lights which I thought were probably its eyes. I could see the veins in the wings of the creature. That is how low it had been over my head. Its body was black all over *and it looked like it was wearing some type of tightly fitted all in one clothing that has the appearance of spandex which had seams that ran down both side of the legs. What really caught my eyes were the boots that it was wearing. They were heavy looking, well made and had extra thick treads on them. The boots had protruding downward facing triangles that were running down the sides of each boot. This creature sure was very strange looking. I had never seen anything like it before. It flew off directly over Newton Abbot town centre and off towards a wooded area where I then lost sight of it. I was left standing shocked, shaking and paralyzed by fear. What had I just witnessed?*

After this incident I have been encountering UFOs and other strange phenomena on a daily basis. I have witnessed things that should not exist. I have photographed many different types of UFOs all across Devon. I have even photographed USOs entering and leaving the sea off the English coast.

In previous reports I have wrongly stated that this incident took place in 1993 but I now know I was mistaken. I found some Polaroid photos that I remember taking days after this incident and they have August 1990 written on the back of them. I now know this incident took place in August of 1990 and I only wish I know the date. All the best." JM

This is quite an interesting account since the witness seems to believe that the winged being was wearing some form of a suit and boots. The part of Devonshire is well-known for UFO activity.

JUNE 10, 2019 IN SHIPPENSBURG, PA

I RECEIVED the following report from Phantoms & Monsters Fortean Research team member Timothy Renner:

"I was wondering if you had heard anything about mothman in the Shippensburg area. Two weeks ago (week of June 10, 2019) my sister was leaving for work around 4:45-5:00 am. She said that she saw a very large black winged creature fly over her car. She said she could clearly see claws on it. She doesn't know I am asking this because she worries about what people would say."

Further information from winged humanoid witness' brother:

"It was three to four feet in body length and a wingspan five to six feet. The body was long and lean, claws on back of legs. Not a bird shaped body. Doesn't think that it had feathers. She said the face was bat-like. Flew very fast. The witness is a birdwatcher, and knows what cranes, hawks, owls look like. She said it reminded her of a crane but it was not a crane. Location was the intersection of Route 11 and Conestoga Drive in Shippensburg, Pa."

Timothy continues to keep tabs on the activity in the area.

SUMMER 2000 NEAR COLONY, MO

I RECEIVED a report from an eyewitness who described a 'hawk-man' entity:

"It was the summer of 2000 in Knox County, Missouri near a small village called Colony. Just north of there is the North Fabius River where there is a concrete bridge. I would fish on this small river, most times underneath the bridge where there was usually a pretty good deep hole to fish.

One night, I was fishing just on the east side of the bridge on the south bank. As I was watching my poles, I heard a loud crashing sound straight across the river from me. It sounded like something was crashing through the trees. I look directly in that direction and saw this large object flying through the air and down to the river. I'm observing enormous wings as this thing lands right in the middle of the river where there is a sandbar that divides two small channels. It lands just to the left of where my line is cast out, maybe twenty feet or so. It was most definitely dark but there was enough light from a burning citronella candle bucket I had burning to where I could see most of the outline of whatever this thing was. I will never forget the size of the wings and how it landed just like a bird. The wings were most likely white or at least light enough where I could make them out pretty easy. It stood on two legs and had the body of a man. The wings were enormous and were taller than the body by a foot or two. It looked mostly naked from what I could tell but I saw some kind of chest straps that went across it's chest. I could not see a face but it looked like it was wearing some kind of helmet and face shield and I say this because it looked exactly like the face shield of the DC comics superhero "Hawkman". It had a pointed face shield that looked like a bird's face and just like the Hawkman character, it had wing-like insignia on its helmet. It looked like a helmet because it appeared to be a different color or shade than its body.

After it had landed, it stood straight up and had its wings tucked in and it didn't move for a very long time. I just kept *staring at it, as I was afraid to move. I can't say how much time passed but it seemed like a long time that I watched it. All of a sudden I saw it moving even more and it looked like it had a large vase in its hand and was dipping it into the water and started pouring water on its right wing. To me it seemed like it must have been injured because of the way it crashed through the trees. That's what it appeared like anyway. After it did that, it stood straight and didn't move at all. It stood there for the longest time and didn't flinch at all. I watched it for at least another twenty to thirty minutes and it did not move. I was scared and I just kept thinking in my mind that it had to be able to see me or at least see the citronella bucket burning. I started to tell myself that what I was seeing wasn't real. I had two poles with me at the time but only one was cast out. I just started reeling it in nice and slow while keeping my eye on this thing.*

All of a sudden I see this thing leap and jump into the water like a dive and water splashes up and there's a wake hitting the bank. I immediately grab my poles and take off running. I kept falling down, scared out of my mind in a total panic thinking this thing was behind me. I finally got past the rocks and onto the road and went straight for the truck. I drove off quickly, still thinking this thing might be following me. I was scared. I was actually scared for a very long time. Looking back now, maybe the creature was just as scared as I was." JP

I contacted the witness by telephone and was assured of what was observed. Very bizarre account.

OCTOBER 11, 2013 NEAR FREEPORT, PA

I RECEIVED A TELEPHONE CALL FROM 'DF' who lives on his farm with his family near Freeport, PA in Armstrong County, PA:

On October 11, 2013, at approximately 5:30 pm, DF was in his recording studio (a separate building on the property). A client was playing the piano at the time. DF walked to the adjoining kitchen to get a glass of water. When he looked out the window he noticed a large winged being descending from the sky. He described it as an 'owlman' with wide feathered wings that had a longer feather spaced six to seven inches along the bottom edge of the wings. The head was round with large black circular eyes, small owl-like ears and a short hooked beak. The body was five foot in height and shaped like that of a human with legs, ending in three-toed talon feet. The feathered body was light to dark tan. The wingspan was eighteen to twenty feet. It was a huge and impressive sight.

The winged being seemed to be drawn by the piano music, in DF's opinion. It landed briefly near the back of the studio, then flapped its wings three times and quickly ascended into the sky. He mentioned the sighting to his wife and children, who said that he should report the encounter.

A few days later, DF was once again in the recording studio. There was another client playing the piano. As DF briefly stepped outside, he noticed the same winged being descending near the studio. This time it must have seen DF as it quickly flew away.

DF is a bit old-school and didn't have a cellphone with him at that time. But he did sketch the winged being after each occasion (displayed below). After six years, he was finally convinced to come forward with his sighting.

I then asked Phantoms & Monsters Fortean Research

member Ryan Fusco to go to the location, talk to the witness and investigate the area. His report is as follows:

"Arriving at our witnesse's location we found out right away that this man was very intelligent, and as you'll soon find out credible as well. DF was able to retell the entire incident, also compensating for the six years of tree growth on his property.

The location has solar panels that power two homes, a barn and a music studio. DF started off by telling us his experience.

The flying beast he saw was between five and six feet tall, a round head with large black circles for eyes, small owl-like ears, very wide feathers and longer feathers attached as a bottom row on the wings, that were anywhere from six to seven inches long. It had a short-hooked beak and had three clawed talon. He also added that it had a yellow gold color to its belly.

After hearing what DF had to say I trusted my instincts and asked if he had seen it more than twice. He said that there was a third incident that occurred between 1:30 and 2 in the morning. He and his wife were woken by a startling sound that resembled a woman screaming mixed with the screeching of an owl. DF ran to the window, opened it up to get a better idea of what the sound was. He described it as "the sound that bones would make rubbing against a metal roof." At first, he thought it was coming from his well house but when he turned his head he realized it was on top of his barn. DF grabbed his bow. But by that time the creature had flown off. At the time, they owned several cats. In the morning their cat Leo was never seen again. DF and his wife swear that the 'owlman' took him.

There have been a couple of sightings of this thing, here and there, by others throughout those six years. A family member of his and their son claims to have seen this creature feeding on a deer carcass on the side of a road.

I was sent to the location to investigate claims that the witness knew where this thing was coming from. DF eventually got a job at a mushroom farm, which was 8 miles east from his location. He was sure that this was a roosting area.

A few local teenager had apparently seen the creature at some point and followed it back to the caves on the farm. These teenagers were caught on the property at night through surveillance cameras. When caught they explained their reason for being there. "There's a giant bat like creature with glowing red eyes that lives in these caves. We've seen it leave and come back several times and we're here to kill it..." Ryan Fusco"

An investigation of this phenomenon will continue.

LATE 1980s NEAR FAYETTEVILLE, WV

On October 3, 2019, I was contacted by 'MJ' in reference to a Mothman encounter in Fayette County, West Virginia:

"Our family lived in Fayetteville, West Virginia and our home was located one-tenth of a mile from the major town street. Our house was located in the forest and our property bordered a state forest. I was 11-12 at the time. The forest was dense with well-worn hiking paths. Some had been logging roads at one time. One was larger as it had once been a rock quarry road. The remains of the quarry was located on our property. A quarter mile from the quarry was a convergence to two creeks. One was Wolf Creek. The convergence point once had a five-foot stone dam that was blasted years before my time due to waterborne disease outbreaks. The town dumped its sewage into the smaller creek. Beyond the convergence of the creek it

descended several large waterfall systems into the New River George. When waters were low a large flat rock creek bed was exposed and we played in it as kids.

Several of us were wrapped up in the Dungeons & Dragons craze, were enamored by heavy metal music and teetered on the edge of occult interests. Nothing too serious. Boys of their time and place. During one late afternoon I proclaimed upon the top of a rock outcrop over the creek bed that I was calling forward a great spirit of the deep forest. Nothing happened. We continued playing until dusk, parted ways and returned home. Perhaps it was happenstance. Perhaps related.

My experience with Mothman began that week and lasted just less than a month. I did not speak of it or share with others for nearly 15 years. I was afraid that speaking of it would somehow cause it to come back around. I will spare you the minor details but need to share the only backstory that matters.

A few years earlier I played with a girl my age and her

younger brother. They had a grand three story wooden home in our neighborhood. It was a historic house, a mansion by local standards. We entered her home one night after searching out fireflies in the front yard. When we walked through the foyer to the main staircase to the second floor I looked to my right across a large sitting room where there were sets of large windows. Outside the windows was a large hardwood about 75 years old. I saw two large red eyes. Large! I stopped. The girl and her brother were already a fourth the way up the stairs and I was standing still and mesmerized. I said, "There are two red eyes in your tree." The girl replied back, "That's a ghost. He has red eyes, looks like an old man, sits in the tree and stares at us sometimes." I asked if they ever called the police. She said no. She said her mom told them not to look at it and ignore it. Their mom often seemed drained and depressed. I was glad I did not have old creepy men sitting in trees around our house. It stayed with me.

Back to my main story. I immediately felt that I was being watched at all times. The primal feeling of prey being stalked. It did not matter if I was in my house, woods, walking to the park, anytime during the day or night. There were scratches at my second floor window but no trees. Deep fear of getting out of bed, paralyzing fear, with many sleepless nights. I tried to share with my parent that strange things were going on, but they had no interest. I would wake them up at night and ask them to search the house, check the doors, etc. They were annoyed. They did agree to keep the flood lights on surrounding the house. My dog was acting strange. Normally a brave dog not scared by bear, not man, nor bigger dog. He was a mess while this was going on.

I called one of my friends that was there with us when we were playing and asked him to come over. That it was very important. I told him I would only speak with him in-person about it. He did and I learned he too was having a series of strange and frightening events. He felt we needed to stick together and tell no one as they would think we were nuts. Needless to say I did spend a lot of time at his house located in a non-wooded neighborhood. The stuff going on at his house was just as bad. Knocking on multiple walls during the day. A thousand birds on the power lines outside his home. The fear of being watched and followed. He was irritated with me as he felt it had been my fault.

One night I mustered the courage to go to my bedroom window and look out on the backyard. A being crossed from the shadows of the house side across the yard and into the flood light lit area just a bit, stopped and looked over its shoulder at me at an upward angle as I was in an elevated position. First, this thing was eight to nine feet tall. Had its giant wings pulled in across its back so that it looked like a cloak. It looked straight ahead again and seemed to glide across the yard in a standing position. It did not have traditional legs and the legs came together into a very strange point, as though its stance could not support its mass yet they did. It used no stride. It was not human.

Many years later, when the film 'The Mothman Prophecies' came out, I was amazed. The static on the phone, headaches, etc, at the time of the events I assumed it was a demon. Mothman was not a term I knew. I never saw it spread its wings or fly. I did have the feeling it was above me. A birds-eye view. The damn thing was silent as I have the hearing of a fruit bat. I had a panic attack that night, cold sweats and felt very alone. I got down on my knees and prayed in a way I never had and never have since.

There was one wise old man who cut our grass and acted as a handyman when the mines closed from time to time. He liked me. Gave me a lot of advice. Told me stories. He had three girls and no boys. My dad liked to do his own work but pitched the fellow work because he was a good guy. He was working on our mower when I broached the subject briefly. He stopped what he was doing, stood up, took me by the shoulders and looked me in the eyes. He said I know what you are talking about. It is the thing we do not talk about in this town. It is called Mothman and even talking about it can bring him around. That was it.

I live in Atlanta now and during 2005 I finally shared the whole story with my wife of six years. Within a week I was in the back courtyard and one swooped. The wingspan and speed was awesome. It perched (not like a bird) seventy yards away at about seventy feet and watched me. No red eyes during the middle of the day and blended well. They do not weigh much but are crazy large, intelligent and not human. It moved on within a week. While they can communicate telepathically, so can I when you lock minds with it. I let it know that it was out of its element in a city like Atlanta, that I had no fear and that I would end it should it mess with my family and property. Not sure I could. But I was a man at that time and had very little patience and refused to succumb to fear. They are most curious about us. They don't think like humans. Don't have the same values and motivations. There were no tragedies associated with my experience. They are voyeurs by nature. I don't think they are physically as strong as a full man. But I can't imagine getting a shot at one." MJ

SEPTEMBER 2018 NEAR HOBBS, NM

I received the following account on January 17, 2020:

"I'm writing this based on what I saw going to work one morning in September 2018. I rather like to stay anonymous. I live on the state line of New Mexico and Texas. I left my home at 4:30 am to head into work in Seminole, TX to open up at 6:00 am. The drive takes about thirty minutes. I always took Rt. 214 to Rt. 3306 all the way to the Seminole Highway. This morning will always be with me, as I turned onto Rt. 3306 maybe a mile or so I see a large man. So I slowed down because I thought it was odd to see a man on the electric pole so early in the morning. But as I got closer, I saw no truck or any indication that someone was servicing the electrical pole. That's when I saw a huge man crouch over with large black feathered wings extending down its back and a bony spine in-between the wings with his head down to his chest. I didn't look back." SS

I contacted the witness and she offered a bit more information. The area of the sighting was in Hobbs, New Mexico, a location with a lot of crude oil pumps. The dark winged humanoid had grasped onto the electrical pole near the top. The winged were definitely feathered and quite large. The body was membraned or bare skin. The head was small and round with no observable features. The witness estimated that the total body length was eight to nine foot.

The witness is of Navajo heritage and they stated that this type of winged being was described to her in the past by their grandfather. He had described it as a form taken by a Skinwalker and that it was a malevolent being. The witness said that there have been large flying beings seen in the area in the past, but they feel that these other sightings were of large birds or Thunderbirds. The witness provided a sketch of the humanoid they observed (below).

The witness was very fearful of receiving ridicule by the

local populace, so it is important to maintain anonymity. The location is approximately fifty miles southeast of Roswell, NM.

SUMMER 2010 – GILROY, CA

I RECEIVED the following account on November 19, 2019:

"Nine years ago I was living along the Uvas Creek in my home town of Gilroy, CA. It was late summer around 12:30 am to shortly after 1:00 am when my two other companions and I heard a screaming sound of death coming farther down from us. I was already planning to go outside to check on my neighbor's tent close to where we heard that high pitched cry of something being killed. The tent was empty like it should be. I started to take the trail back to my spot. It wasn't very dark due to the fact that the moon was going to be full. I was almost in front of my spot when I heard the sound of air three times - woosh, woosh, woosh.

I turned towards the creek and looked at the bend not expecting to see what I saw. From behind the trees and shrubs was a black devilish gargoyle that was eight to ten feet in length. It was red-eyed, red-mouthed with bat-like wings. Its skin was dense rubbery looking. It was gliding past me, not knowing I was watching it. In my head I repeated don't look at me, don't look at me, over and over staying perfectly still. It continues to glide past. My friend, who was looking for me said, 'what are you doing?' I said, 'come here, come here.' He sees the back of it and said, 'WTF was that?'

Finally, this year 2019, four other local witnesses say they have also seen it in the past 6 months. The thing that really bothers me is how could it stay up in the air only flapping its wigs three times? It was huge! No way! It's impossible. It was going too slow to stay up, BUT IT DID! I know what I saw that night and nothing is going to change my mind." SB

MID-1990S NEAR GLEN CARBON, IL

I received the following account on December 5, 2019:

"I just read your recent article and I'd like to report that my husband and I witnessed what we have called a "human vampire bat thing" for years.

We live in Edwardsville, IL, and were driving home from an event in St. Louis late one night. Unfortunately, I don't know the date, but believe it was a work Christmas party, so that time of year. It was some time after 1988 when we built our current house and before 1996 before our son was born (we think). For sure after 1988 but it's possible our son was at a sitter. We were on Hwy. 270 between IL Route 157 and IL Route 159 in Glen Carbon, IL, traveling east. A human-sized thing flying west swooped down like it was going to crash into our windshield and then over the top of our car. It was all black with huge wings and/or a cape and it did have a face similar to a human and it seemed to look at us. It happened quickly. Neither of us could believe our eyes and didn't see where it went from there.

We slowed down and looked in our rear view mirrors but never saw it again. Of course, no one believed us!

Then a few years ago, maybe three to four, I saw an article about human-size bats in the Philippines that really did look like what we saw.

So much we don't know about this big crazy world in which we live!" LS

I contacted LS by telephone. After our discussion, I believe the sighting occurred during the mid-1990s. This location is in southern Illinois, an area well-known for flying cryptids and UFO activity. LS described the wings as membrane-like that of a bat and the span at least as wide as the car, about eight to ten feet. The incident occurred around 11:30-midnight. The being descending quickly from the sky and was first noticed because of the highway lights and then the car's headlights. LS estimates that the winged humanoid was approximately five to six feet from the windshield before it instantly ascending over the roof of the car. The body shape was similar to a five to six foot thin human with possible legs and arms, though it was difficult to gauge the length and size. The winged humanoid that LS referred to in The Philippines was a supposed sighting of an Aswang, some of which have been described as having wings.

DECEMBER 2017 – GILA RIVER INDIAN COMMUNITY, AZ

ON SEPTEMBER 30, 2019 I received the following account:

"I had a sighting of a very large bat creature. I was traveling not far from my home on the reservation where I noticed something flickering in the sky. Then this thing appeared about two hundred feet in front of my car, standing about twelve feet tall with a wingspan of the entire width of the road. It was grayish brown in color and it had red glowing eyes, as bright as a brake light on a car. It looked at us snarling with long knife like teeth. It took one step, didn't flap it wings and took off into the air. I was glad I had my friend with me because that assured me it was real. I drew a picture of the creature. I can send if you like. I live in Arizona (Gila River

Indian Community) and this happened about 4:00 in the morning in Dec. 2017." JB

I contacted JB in order to gather a few more details. The Gila River Indian Community is located south of Phoenix, Arizona. The drawing is depicted to the right.

6

WINGED CRYPTIDS - PTEROSAURS

In August 2013, cryptozoologist and pterosaur researcher / investigator Jonathan David Whitcomb submitted an article for me to post in 'Phantoms & Monsters':

Why Believe in Living Pterosaurs?
by Jonathan David Whitcomb

I AM grateful for the Phantoms & Monsters report in the July 16, 2013, post *"Pterodactyl-Like Cryptid Witnessed Near the Pine Barrens."* Most eyewitnesses of apparent pterosaurs tell nobody about their strange encounters, except maybe one or two close friends or family members.

I'm also grateful to Lon Strickler for allowing me here to report a few sightings of apparent pterosaurs, but it deserves a brief introduction. This is a strange investigation in a narrow branch of cryptozoology.

Before introducing you to live-pterosaurs (LP) credibility, let me make this plea. Are you one of those few lucky (or unlucky) persons who has seen something like a "pterodactyl" or any large featherless flying creature that was unlike a bat? If something like a winged monster has flown into your life experience, it does not throw your sanity into doubt. It's OK, you're not alone. And do not doubt yourself; believe that the world of life is bigger than what has been portrayed to us in Western culture.

I'm probably the only person in the world who has devoted anything close to a full-time effort, during the past nine years, to interviewing eyewitnesses and analyzing and writing about their testimonies. I will respect you and be open to what you tell me.

You can skip ahead to the end ("A Few Recent Sightings") if you're not interested in technical details about credibility and you already know about the 1944 sighting by Duane Hodgkinson.

This post examines four kinds of credibility issues:

1. Identity
2. Honesty
3. Correlation
4. Extinction Assumption

To the best of my knowledge, this is the first time this subject, of the four basic types of credibility, has been explored in any book or web page or scientific paper, at least regarding the concept of eyewitness reports of apparent pterosaurs.

But first I need to introduce myself.

WHO IS JONATHAN WHITCOMB?:

I WAS a forensic videographer in the fall of 2003, sometimes videotaping injured persons and interviewing their caregivers. I had a personal interest, at the time, in reports of living dinosaurs and pterosaurs, and I made some inquiries. It was like a hobby at first but it soon grew to a big part of my life.

Paul Nation, of Granbury, Texas, sent me a few home videos from two expeditions on a tropical island in Papua New Guinea. I examined the videotaped interviews of natives who had encountered the "ropen" of Umboi Island, and their credibility amazed me. I came to believe those natives were telling the truth.

I would have been even more amazed if I had known that in one year I myself would be camped out on top of a hill in the middle of Umboi Island, hoping that a giant pterosaur would fly down at night and grab the big dead lizard hanging from a small tree, within videotaping distance of the door of my tent. But that's another story. We need to see why searches for living pterosaurs do not come from delusions, why there is reason in the apparent madness.

We need to understand the four basic types of LP credibility; But let's begin with a key sighting, Duane Hodgkinson's encounter during World War II.

1944 Sighting in New Guinea:

THIS MUST BE the most famous "pterodactyl" sighting of the past hundred years. I place it on a pedestal as one of the four key sightings in the Southwest Pacific. So much has been written about it that we'll examine only a few details here.

Two Americans soldiers were stationed in Finschhafen, New Guinea, on the mainland of the largest tropical island in the world. At that time in 1944, no Japanese were left in that area, so the two men were granted permission to hike up to a local village to the west.

In a jungle clearing about one hundred feet in diameter, they both witnessed something huge take off into the air. Duane Hodgkinson, then a weather observer for the artillery, described the encounter to me six decades later. My cryptozoology associate Garth Guessman also interviewed him.

The creature ran through the grass, with long legs clearly not to be confused with the long tail. Hodgkinson could see that the legs, during the running takeoff, were about three to four feet long. He estimated the tail to be "at least ten or fifteen feet long." He was certain that he had not confused the legs for a tail.

But Hodgkinson was concentrating on the head, especially

on the long appendage that was like a horn, held parallel to the long neck of the "pterodactyl."

The wingspan appeared to him to be the same as that of a private airplane. He would later own a Piper Tri-pacer and he considered its wingspan (29 feet) to be very similar to that of the flying creature that he had encountered west of Finschhafen in 1944.

The Four Types of LP Credibility:

HODGKINSON'S SIGHTING report scores very high on the first two types of credibility, and only those two types relate directly to individual sighting reports. The third and fourth types relate to overall sighting reports and the overall concept of pterosaur extinction or non-extinction.

Credibility Type One: Identity

WHEN SOMEBODY REPORTS A FLYING creature that looked like a pterosaur, did it actually have those characteristics? A common kind of question that a skeptic might ask is "Was it a misidentification? Could it have been a bird or a bat that was seen in unusual conditions?"

Another variation of that credibility type is this: Could it have been a hallucination? We might also ask, "Could it have been a combination of imagined details?"

The report by Hodgkinson indicates the animal was huge and seen at close range, probably less than a hundred feet away. Examining the details makes it obvious: No bird or bat was involved. Here's why: If a bird was running, during takeoff, much closer to the two soldiers than Hodgkinson thought was the distance, it could have been much smaller, with a wingspan less than twenty-nine feet. But why would a bird (just a few yards away or so) look like a featherless "pterodactyl" with a very long tail and a sharp horn coming out the back of the head? And why would it look like slow wing flaps that blow around the grass in the clearing?

Another critical point needs to be examined. After the creature had flown out of sight, it returned, flying over the clearing in the opposite direction. The two men then watched it again fly out of sight. If they had been startled at the takeoff, and had some kind of delusion of "pterodactyl" features, they would have seen their mistake when it flew back over the clearing; they would have seen that it was really only a bird.

But nothing had changed in its appearance during that brief time when the creature had been out of sight. It was still a huge pterosaur or at least a huge flying creature that had characteristics commonly associated with pterosaurs.

The possibility that two men, at the same time, hallucinated a huge pterosaur---that is too unlikely to deserve attention. And we need to remember that it would have had to have been two hallucinations, for the flying creature returned after being out of sight. Forget about that explanation.

For credibility Type One, the 1944 Finschhafen sighting report is very strong.

Credibility Type Two: Honesty

THIS IS SIMPLE. Did the person reporting a living pterosaur lie about the experience? (We need to be careful not to confuse Type Two with a subset of Type Three below.) Some skeptics speculate about the hoax possibility, especially by proclaiming that natives are making up stories for gullible Americans. But that speculation is weak.

None of those skeptics, as far as I know, have ever gone on any expedition to Papua New Guinea (or anywhere else) to test their idea by interviewing natives themselves. On the other hand, my associates and I have interviewed natives while video-taping them, giving investigators opportunities to judge eyewitness honesty themselves.

Why do I judge the 1944 Hodgkinson sighting report as very high in honesty credibility? I don't usually give away many details about my methods of judging honesty, for I don't want to make it easy for a future hoaxer to use that to fool me. But with Hodgkinson, I can disclose something that is no secret anyway.

Duane Hodgkinson has been a flight instructor for many years, near Livingston, Montana. He needs to be credible to clients. Holding onto an old story about his view of a giant pterodactyl could hurt his credibility, if it were a made up story. He holds firm to his account because it was a true experience. Those friends who have dismissed it with "what were you drinking?"---those friends have not caused Hodgkinson to abandon his account. (By the way, this World War II veteran has never been a drinker.)

Let's now leave the first two types of credibility, the individual- report focuses, and look at numbers three and four, the overall- credibility issues.

Credibility Type Three: Correlation

MANY FACTORS CAN BE COMPARED in sighting reports, too many to examine them all right now. Consider a subset we can call "hoax potential," not to be confused with Type Two above. We now look at the possibility that has been brought up by some skeptics, or at least implied: that sightings in general are made up of a significant number of hoaxes.

Let's call this one "Subtype 3-A." Could a sighting be a hoax? A precise answer may not be possible, for a clever hoaxer might squeeze one fabricated report into a compilation of sighting accounts, however much we try to keep the data clean from hoaxes.

This is not about honesty in an individual sighting, however (like Type Two); it's about all the sightings (Subtype 3-A) and how some could be hoaxes.

Is there a significant number of hoaxes in the overall reports?

Analysis of the overall data answers that question: No, there is not.

At the end of 2012, I finished compiling data from 128 sighting reports. Those 128 I chose because they appeared to me to be more likely than not from actual encounters with modern pterosaurs.

How does that compilation relate to hoax possibilities? Several things demonstrate that few, if any, hoaxes could be included in those 128 reports.

Consider a simple example: eyewitness belief that the creature seen was featherless. The data shows that 21% of the eyewitnesses were positive about the absence of feathers, and 25% thought there were no feathers but admitted some doubt.

That 21% to 25% difference demonstrates that no significant number of hoaxes could be included in those 128 reports. If many hoaxes were involved, those reporting the lies would not have admitted any doubt about the lack of feathers, and the overall percentages would have been very different, with the reported beliefs about lack of feathers.

Wingspan estimates also show that few, if any, hoaxes were involved, but let's move on to the fourth general type.

Credibility Type Four: Extinction Assumption

IN CONTRAST to the first three types, this one usually involves doubting the validity of sighting reports. It's used by skeptics as if it were a trump card. I use the phrase "universal-extinction axiom," regarding pterosaurs and dinosaurs.

This could be covered well in a book, but we need to be brief. It means that the extinction of all species of dinosaurs and pterosaurs has been an idea so deeply entrenched in Western society that it is now mostly taken for granted as part of "science."

But a survey of American biology professors, a few months ago, resulted in a surprising outcome. Although few professors replied to the questionnaire, the average percentage of belief was 1.5% regarding the possibility of a modern living pterosaur. And those were professors who apparently had no previous knowledge that anybody was investigating the possibility of extant pterosaurs.

Of course 1.5% is a very small estimate of the probability that a pterosaur species is alive; but it's clearly more than zero.

In addition, when a typical paleontologist is pressed for an answer to a question about the possibility of an extant pterosaur species, the response is usually that such a thing is possible but unlikely.

So the extinction of all species of pterosaurs is not actually a scientific fact. It is just a popular idea. That means this Type Four cannot be used as if it were a trump card against other types of credibility.

A Few Recent Sightings:

LET'S look at excerpts from a few recent sighting reports, and I'll include a brief general evaluation of each one, regarding the first two credibility types.

On March 23, 2013, a man was driving on Interstate-540, on the north side of Raleigh, North Carolina, at about sunset, when something strange flew right in front of his car. With a wingspan of about five to six feet, a long tail that ended in a "spade," a crest on its head, something like claws in mid-wing, and a complete lack of feathers, it gave him a shock. I rate this as high in both Type One and Type Two credibility.

In northern Minnesota, three eyewitnesses saw a creature "gliding across the highway." This could have been as recently as early 2011; the report I received did not give a date or exact location. The flying creature had "reddish brown leather type skin with no feathers, bat like wings, a crest on its head, a mouth full of small teeth in the back and larger in the front . . ." It also had long legs and a long tail: both legs and tail, no confusion apparent between them. The tail had "a spade shaped thing at the end of it." I rate this as high in Type One and average in Type Two credibility.

On November 14, 2012, Professor Steven Watters saw a "huge rhamphorhynchus like flying entity" gliding past his house, at 11:45 a.m., in Crestview, Florida. He estimated the wingspan at eight to twelve feet and he told me that it had "a tail as long as its torso with a large bulb" at the end of the tail: "very diamond shaped, no feathers . . ."

He checked out photos of Frigate birds and was sure that was not what he had observed. The "rhamphorhynchus" had a neck and Professor Watters observed that Frigate birds appear to have not neck at all. I rate this as high in both Type One and Type Two.

Many other reports could be given but let's leave them for a future post.

NOTE: I sincerely thank Jonathan Whitcomb for submitting this excellent information. I have been extremely interested in his research since he started researching the 'ropen' in New Guinea. Lon

OCTOBER 22, 2002 –SHELL ISLAND NATURE PRESERVE, FL

I received a report from 'AL' who is a college degree holder in Anthropology and who conducted field investigation for MUFON in the late 80s and into mid 90s:

"We were vacationing in Panama City Beach, Florida and had decided to boat out to Shell Island Nature Preserve arriving just an hour before Sunset. Sunset came and went and just before darkness began to fall we returned to the boat which we had to wade to from shore. We had to drop anchor twenty feet off shore for fear of getting caught on a sand bar. This was October 22, 2002. Clear day in the 80s. As we waded out to the boat and were getting in, we saw the craziest sight. All the birds and wildlife took off at once and scattered in every direction from the spot we had just come. The sound and sight immediately drew our full attention. We then observed the thing waddle out from the bush! This was a small one seven to eight feet tall (judging from the bush height along the shore). Our cameras were in the boat since we had gone to Shell Island for a little metal detecting beach combing.

It looked directly at us and paced back and forth along the shore for approximate distance of thirty feet in total. We didn't wait around to get a better view of it, once we saw the head crest.

It was a Pterosaur, period!

If the sightings only happened in the USA on one or two occasions then I can understand the tendency to dismiss the reports as those of remote controlled engineering creations causing confusion for any unwitting observers. But this isn't the case. There are hundreds of these documented sightings. It's close to unbelievable in the mainstream modern western world but the evidence suggests that a bizarre creature which once mimicked a Pterosaur millions of years ago has out-lived it's prehistoric companion. These sightings ARE REAL." AL

APRIL 2012 – CENTRAL ARKANSAS

In November 2014 I received the following report from a witness in Central Arkansas:

"I decided that I needed to go to the grocery store to pick up a few things. I was out in the country, driving slowly, all alone, going over a bridge at about 2 pm on a sunny springtime afternoon in April 2012, when all of the sudden I see something coming up from underneath the bridge.

From out of the passenger seat window and about five or six feet from me I can see something medium gray. As it came up a little bit more I could see part of a wing, part of a beak, part of a head crest, and a big gold eye. It looked as if it was struggling to get up over that bridge and up over my truck because of its heavy weight.

As I slowed down even more and looked at it closely the first thought to enter my mind was 'prehistoric' and my second thought was 'it looks like something that shouldn't still be living today'. My third thought was 'prehistoric bird.'

I then watched out the windshield as it flew up over my truck, up into the sky, and off toward a wooded area, southward. It seemed as if everything was in slow motion as I watched it fly up above my truck and fly away. I watched its wings above me and how they looked and moved. They moved like a muscular wave from one end of the wing to the tip. The wings were thick like a steak, were shaped like an airplane's wings. The wings had three sections to them, with black creases or wrinkles running down them. And on the middle outside of the wings were what looked like fringes (which I found out later were claws or fingers).

I then noticed the torso, how big in was and that it was shaped kind of like an egg. I observed the head crest and how strange it looked on top of the head and how it kind of bounced up and down as the creature flew. I also noticed the long length of the neck. The legs just floated in the air and kind of bounced on each side of the tail. The tail had a heart looking shape at the end of it. The beast had no feathers and that it was probably as big as a small airplane, and bigger than my little Chevy S10 pickup.

I was in some kind of shock the rest of the day, just walking around and trying to function in some kind of a daze, going through the motions but only really half way there. My mind was trying to come to terms with what I had seen.

I contacted two of my friends who suggested that what I had really seen was a Heron, Albatross, Pelican or some local big bird, even though I told them that this creature was huge, not big and had no feathers at all.

An internet search under 'prehistoric birds' produced several posts about Pterosaurs. I didn't really know what Pterosaurs were but I knew that they weren't birds and that they didn't exist any longer (or so I thought). So I became discouraged and gave up until early 2013." LD

The witness later forwarded the following information after she talked to Jonathan David Whitcomb:

"Subject: Guesstimates, measurements, estimates

I could come up with some measurements as to the size of the creature. But coming up with the measurements of the tail is the hardest. It was a short-tailed Pterosaur. Here are the measurements I have:

1. *Wings from tip of one wing to tip of the other: no smaller than fourteen foot (maybe longer).*
2. *Face, bill and eye to the end of (tip) the head crest: three to three and a half foot long (the head crest was shaped like the prongs of a household hammerhead (kind of a horn with a curve in it).*
3. *The whole animal from the tip of its head to the tip of its tail was probably nine to twelve foot long.*
4. *Its eye was no smaller than five inches around.*
5. *Its torso was probably four to five foot long and shaped kind of like a lemon, only longer (an elongated lemon).*
6. *Even though the tip of the Pterosaurs left wing was five or six foot from me as it was coming up beside my truck I could not see the tail until it was up in the air and above my truck. I want to say that the tail was two or three foot long.*

I remember the tail being just slightly longer than the feet as it was flying above me. It was the tail flange that was a little longer than the feet. The feet where like claws or talons floating in the air behind the creature. And the tail had a spade shaped flange at the end of it.

It looked to be about the size of small airplane and bigger than my Chevy S10." LD

I have no doubt that the witness encountered a Pterosaur or a creature very similar to it. As you read on, there is mounting evidence that the phenomenon may be real.

SPRING 2013 – VERMILLION RIVER IN DANVILLE, IL

I RECEIVED a telephone call from an eyewitness who was referred to me by an associate.

In the spring of 2013, DF was on his property at the end of Ave. F, near the Vermilion River in Danville, Illinois. It was around 4 pm on a warm sunny afternoon. The property extended back to the edge of the river. DF was busy clearing brush and trees on the bluff overlooking the river. Many times, he would ride his ATV to the location, then sit and watch a variety of wildlife along a game trail. There was also a dock on the property.

On that day, DF was taking a break from his work. After a while, he noticed that the regular sound of birds had suddenly stopped, and it became usually quiet. DF said that he has always been very quick to pick-up on movement, since he has ridden a motorcycle and needed to be aware of his surroundings.

As he stood on the bluff looking out onto the river, he noticed a large shadowy figure gliding downstream towards him. As it got closer, the bizarre creature became more defined. He observed, what he described, a 'pterodactyl' gliding about four to five feet above the surface of the river. DF estimated that the wingspan was approximately twenty-five feet, as it covered half the width of the river.

The huge flying being looked exactly like the images of the prehistoric flying dinosaur. Long beak with a long ray on the head. Dark gray leathery-skinned body and wings, with a long tail that flattened on the end. It made little sound but cast a shadow on the river as it flew just below the height of the bluff. The water swirled as it glided past. The beast continued gliding downstream until DF lost sight of it. He stated that it never flapped its wings. DF's first reaction was to get back to his house and tell his wife what he had seen.

Over the years, he mentioned the sighting to a few close friends, but it never went beyond that. He moved from the location about a year later.

I was impressed by DF's demeanor and description. He stated that he has never witnessed anything unusual before or since that day. Historically, much of Illinois is known for flying cryptids sightings. While investigating the Chicago winged humanoid reports, our team also received a variety of flying cryptids sightings as well, including pterosaurs and large-winged birds. Danville is approximately 100 miles south of Chicago, near the Indiana border.

SPRING 2001 NEAR MOBILE, AL

"What I saw that day changed by life and I have never made an official report until today. Around midday spring of 2001, I left my home to attend college classes. We lived down a single lane dirt road in the outskirts of Mobile, Alabama near a large water reservoir called Big Creek Lake. I had the windows of my car down as it was a beautiful day. The radio was off and because of the dirt road, I was driving slowly. I heard a strange

noise overhead coming towards me and it piqued my curiosity enough to stop my car and try to see what it was. We lived near a Coast Guard base, so helicopters and other small planes were not unusual to see. But when I heard the noise again, I realized it was unlike anything I had ever heard.

As I leaned my head out the open window, a shadow covered my car and the entire road. Above was the underside of a dark grey leathery animal whose sleek, muscular body carried two enormous bony wings. As it soared over me at a very low height just above the tree line, the body came to a point. I am unsure if there was a tail or just legs arranged in a linear fashion. In an instant, the shadow was gone. All sight of the animal was lost due to surrounding trees. But I heard the noise again. That is when I realized what it was. The sound of air being moved by those gigantic wings. I heard the wings flap a couple more times in what seemed like an impossible wait time between; then, nothing. I sat in disbelief.

I did a bit of research, and it closely resembled a Pterosaur or flying prehistoric dinosaur. I believe that anything is possible in this weird world. I know what I saw. I will never forget it." MB

EARLY SPRING 2016 – GARY, IN

I RECEIVED the following report by email on January 23, 2019. I followed-up with a telephone call:

"Sir, I had the experience of seeing this big grayish prehistoric bird. It was 7:40 in the morning on a clear sunny day. I was driving down Broadway in Gary, right across from the gas station right before you get on the exit at I-65 South. I was *shocked, wandering why no one else noticed this creature. The beak was pointy, and the wings were quite long. The wings did not flap. The creature flew low enough for me to just look up, and there it was.*

At first, I thought that I was seeing things, so I waited a couple of days before I told my husband. I don't drink, or do drugs, so I know what I saw.

After a couple of weeks, I saw it again in the same area, but not the same spot. Also, this one was smaller creature. It did not look like a bat, or an owl. I Googled 'prehistoric birds,' and there I saw the best picture to describe what I saw. After that I looked up at the sky often but hadn't seen it again. I also thought about reporting it, but people of course would think that I was crazy. It came to me that woody, dense areas is where they hide." PC

I called PC immediately after receiving her email. She gave me the exact location of the sighting, an area near a gas station that once had a thick grove of trees in the vicinity. The trees have since been cleared. This is in the area of W 37th Ave east-bound between Broadway and I-65.

This sighting occurred in the late spring / early summer of 2016. PC had just taken her children to school and saw the creature on her way home. She stated that the creature was quite large. The body was approximately the length of a van and the wings had a width at least double the length. PC is positive that this was a Pterosaur-like being, after looking for an example online.

A few days later, her friend also observed this creature. Her husband witnessed a similar creature several weeks later. I'm sure that other residents in the area were aware of the presence of these creatures at the time but were fearful of reporting their sightings.

PC's husband's friend told him about the recent Gary, Indiana sightings, and she decided to contact me. I'm not discounting that this may have been a remote-controlled device, though the size and the general socio-economic area is puzzling, if that is the case. The team was following up on this incident, along with all previous and subsequent encounters.

JULY 5, 2019 – WHEATON, IL

I RECEIVED a telephone call from a witness 'KM' who described the sighting of a cryptid winged creature.

KM was driving on Jewell Rd., about a half mile west of Gary Ave. in Wheaton, Illinois during the late afternoon of July 5, 2019. He had been helping a friend with a yard sale.

As KM was looking ahead of him, he noticed a strange form flying in the sky at an altitude of approximately two hundred feet. The profile was that of a Pterosaur, a long tail with a 'spade' on the end. The head was indistinguishable because of the angle, but the wings were wide and comparable to the classic form. The creature was dark in color and propelled itself with slow deliberate wing flaps.

KM was able to observe the winged creature for fifteen to twenty seconds and is positive that it was not a crane or heron, of which he is very familiar with. The wingspan was undetermined, but much wider than any known indigenous bird.

This is a continuation of cryptid bird and winged humanoid sightings in the Upper Midwest, especially throughout the state of Illinois and Indiana.

7

WINGED CRYPTIDS – DRAGONS

JULY 3, 2016 NEAR TUCKAHOE, NJ

On July 19, 2016 I received the following account from a witness in New Jersey:

"Hello - last weekend I was driving on Marshallville Rd. by the river near Tuckahoe, NJ. I don't know the time, but it was dusk, and the sky was light enough to see anything in the sky.

I caught a glimpse of a huge flying creature crossing the roadway approximately a hundred feet in the air. I swear it was shaped like a dragon and silhouetted against the lighter sky. It was flying south towards the state forest.

I looked at it for almost ten seconds. The wings were wide and there was a long tail. The head was like that of an unknown reptile. It was dark in color and flapped the giant wings, which had to be thirty feet or more in width. There was another car behind me. They surely saw it by the expression on their faces. I pulled over and the two people in the other car looked over when they passed me, pointing to the sky. I tried to get them to stop but they were moving by too fast. I lowered by window and yelled but they continued driving. When I stuck my head out of the window, I immediately smelled a foul stench and felt warm down drafts. It was very weird.

I'm not naive and I know that this could not have been an actual animal. I almost feel like I entered a time warp at the time this creature appeared. For the rest of the evening I had a physical reaction comparable to jet lag.

I haven't said anything to anyone else. I live alone and retired. I've lived in this area for most of my life and I've never experienced anything like this. There has been no mention of this in the local news. I may have seen something I shouldn't have.

Sir, what are your thoughts?" Malcolm

I called Malcolm and we had an interesting conversation. He asked me to redact some personal information in his original email since I asked for his permission to publish. I gathered a few additional details. The sighting date was Sunday, July 3, around 8:15 pm. His description was stark and believable. The body from tip to tail was estimated at fifty to sixty feet and that there were two long appendages on each side of the head. The foul stench was likened to rotting fish.

We discussed his assertion of a possible time slip. I asked if he noticed other changes in the surrounding area during the sighting. He said that didn't detect other anomalies. I conducted a follow-up investigation on this sighting.

MID-1980S IN HAMILTON, NJ

On July 25, 2016, I received a response after posting the earlier sighting account in New Jersey:

"Hi, I just read your post about the dragon sighted over

southern New Jersey. It took me by surprise because I had a similar experience in the mid-eighties when I was still a kid (about ten years old, I think).

It was before noon, in the springtime, and I was biking around a local ballpark by my house. (Nottingham baseball field in Hamilton, NJ). There were no games scheduled that day so I was alone, as far as I could tell.

There was a play area and a pond by the woods that I would frequent when I was bored, in the hopes of finding other kids to play with.

About halfway there, while looking up at the clouds and sky, I saw what I thought was a plane coming from the south. There's a small air strip by us and there were some very cool biplanes that would fly by from time to time. My favorite was a Red Baron style one, and I thought that was it, because of the color.

I stopped and turned to watch (and wave). When the plane gave its wings a single long flap, that's when I realized it wasn't a plane.

It was a dragon. There is no doubt in my mind. It was dark red, and I could see the sun shimmering off its scales as it got closer. I felt frozen to the spot, dumbstruck, a little scared, and very excited.

It was huge, flying at about the same height as the biplanes do, and it didn't make any sound as it went overhead. It was just gliding. It was like a classical European dragon, but the proportions were a little different.

When it was right overhead, I felt a blast of heat. I assumed it was its fiery breath at the time. I was absolutely vibrating with excitement and looking around frantically for anyone else that might be around. The ballfields were empty, and no one was outside in the nearby houses.

It kept going at a steady clip and right before it

disappeared over the tree line to the north it gave another slow flap of its massive wings.

I turned right around and sped out of the park hoping to find someone else who saw it too. Everyone was inside their homes that early. When I got home, I realized no one would believe me. So, I never told my parents. They'd think I was making it up. Instead I told my older sister, but she said I probably saw a hang-glider or a fancy plane.

It was such an odd sighting and I never perused it further." D

MARCH 2013 / OCTOBER 2015 NEAR VOORHEES, NJ

I RECEIVED another New Jersey sighting account on October 17, 2016:

Hello, I just read about that flying dragon over south New Jersey in 'Weird NJ.' I had a very similar experience twice.

First time was about three years ago in March. I was driving near Marlton, NJ and the Voorhees area at around 3:00 pm, looked up and saw this huge creature flying. I was in complete shock because I could not believe the size of this thing and the sun was still out at the time, so I had a pretty good look at it. It was no bird because it did not have feathers or fur. These gigantic wings look like a huge bat with a reptilian head. Exactly how the other person described it in the other report. I was in the car with family and by the time I could get a word out of my mouth and point at it, it had already flown away. Its skin color was like a light beige and it didn't even flap its wings. Kind of just glided. It was flying very low as well, almost resembled a massive Pterodactyl.

The second sighting was in Voorhees. Again, I was driving home at night last year around 9:00 pm October 30. I saw the same exact body shape but slightly smaller and flying lower than the first one. Strange thing was that its eyes glowed this crazy bright red. Like car lights. The eyes on it freaked me out so much I couldn't tell anyone for at least two days. This one also had a darker skin tone or maybe it was just the time of day I saw it. I had a very good look at both creatures. I'm very aware of all the animals that live around me. This is not like anything I have ever seen. I did not experience any foul scents because I did not roll down my window or exit my car. Just wanted to share my part. Maybe it will help your investigation." RF

I called the witness and verified what they had seen. I originally thought that this may have been a huge Pterosaur, but I was convinced that this sighting was much different. After receiving these three accounts, I believe that it may be possible that supposed Jersey Devil witnesses are observing smaller versions of winged reptiles or Pterosaurs. It's food for thought.

SUMMER 2012 – SOUTHWEST FLORIDA

I RECEIVED the following information in March 2018:

"Since you all are into the 'strange,' I'd like to tell you about something I witnessed about six years ago, here in Florida. I was staying with some friends and always go out every night to check on the evening sky. I went out on this one night and looked up to see something that made me look away and rub

my eyes. It was so amazing! But when I looked back, it was still there! Where I stood on the dark driveway, the moon was directly overhead, and circling around it, in a clockwise direction (from my perspective) were what looked like flying dragons! From the languid swoop of their wings, they had to be enormous! But they were all black, silhouetted, with the moon above them, and I could see no colors or details.

Then, I realized that above them were dozens and dozens of tiers of more flying dragons, all circling in the same direction! There were easily over a hundred of those dreadful-looking beings, which I believe were Reptilians, as the 'royal' ones have enormous wings. I estimate that the lowest one was approximately five hundred feet in altitude, though it's difficult to say exactly. And I began to wonder if they could see me down below, as I watched them, which was not a very comforting thought. I wanted to run to get my friends to see all this, but I was afraid of what I might miss.

Then I noticed to the right of them, an enormous black circular craft, slowly and silently approaching the creatures. It was easily a dozen times the width of the moon and all around its rim, was a black, curling, wispy mist. Very slowly the craft crept closer and closer to the circling beings, until it had completely obscured them, as well as the moon. It never stopped or slowed down and remained totally silent. And after it cleared the place where the dragons flew, the sky was empty, save for the gibbous moon and the cold stars. As I watched it move off into the black night, I realized it could never be seen, being so quiet and hidden.

My theory about what had happened is that, you know how when people are out boating, they will sometimes jump into the water for a refreshing swim? Well, I believe the Reptilians had left their craft to stretch those terrible wings, and were circling there, waiting for it to catch up with them, to *get back on board. That's just my theory, because who knows what wicked mischief they'd really been up to? I told my friends what I'd seen, and being the skeptics, they said it was probably bats or birds. But I know what bats and birds look like, and what I saw was something I'd never seen before, or since.*

For days after that event, I worried they might return to do some harm to me, for spying on them. And it's a creepy feeling to think what might be there in the black, night sky, just out of our sight. Thanks for letting me tell my experience and keep trekking into the mystic." KL

The witness did not give a specific location, so I reached out to them. The location was in Sarasota County, Florida and it occurred in the summer of 2012. In the past, I have received other references to flying beings accompanied by a craft-like UFO, as well as other strange phenomenon, from this part of Florida. It was an interesting observation and stylish description, though I believe the presence of a multitude of huge winged beings would have drawn more attention from other witnesses. I have not yet heard or read of any related accounts.

AUGUST 2018 / JANUARY 2019 – CAPAY VALLEY, CA

ON SUNDAY, March 24, 2019, I received a call from a female witness who states that she and a friend encountered a huge flying cryptid while leaving the Cache Creek Casino Resort in Capay Valley, California. The incident occurred in early August 2018, at approximately 11 pm local time.

The witness states that they had just pulled onto Rt. 16 when this Cessna sized 'dragon' swiftly glided over the back towards the front of their vehicle. The winged being was so big that they felt the vehicle shudder from the force of it passing over them. Because of the lights surrounding the area, the witness states that she got an excellent view of the creature. She said that the wings were bat-like and had an approximate span of thirty foot or so. The body was thin and almost human-like. The color was dark, probably black. She also stated that it looked back at them as it flew over and that it had large bright yellow eyes. The witness never saw it flap its wings, but it glided with ease and speed. It quick ascended into the darkness.

The same witness also stated that a friend was at the same location on the first week of January 2019 and witnessed a very similar winged being. This was in the parking lot of the Cache Creek Casino Resort at around 1 am. Their description was of a very large winged entity that quickly passed over head as they were walking to their vehicle. They also felt a slight rush of air as it flew above them.

I asked a friend who lives in the area to see what they could find concerning this supposed 'dragon.' Apparently, this being has been seen on other occasions. The witnesses include a few employees of casino. When my friend asked people about the winged being, some refused to acknowledge the question, while others acted fearful. I plan to continue investigating the phenomena.

8

WINGED CRYPTIDS - WEIRD / MASSIVE BIRDS

JUNE 2014 – MAGOG, QUEBEC, CANADA

In September 2014 I received an interesting cryptid bird encounter report from a witness in Quebec, Canada:

"Hello - thanks for reading my email. I live in a recently built house in Magog, Quebec about one kilometer, west of Lake Magog. Near my house is a forest and large marshy area that is approximately two hundred meters beyond my property. I have lived here for two years. Many of my neighbors have been here the same amount of time.

Since June of this year, we have been hearing loud snarling sounds coming from the marsh, mostly late at night. At first, I thought it may be a coyote or other canine of some kind, but recently we've noticed activity that rules this out.

My neighbor three houses down had recently obtained a llama and kept it in a large railed pen behind their house. This past weekend, the llama disappeared. The only evidence found were drag marks in the area around the pen leading to the marsh. There were no tracks or blood anywhere. In fact, the police took a report and searched. They found nothing.

On Sunday night, I was in my greenhouse cleaning up when I heard a loud thud come from behind my utility shed. I started to walk out of my greenhouse when I heard that distinctive snarling sound and it was very close. I immediately went back into the greenhouse, cut off the lights and quietly watched. I called my wife on my cell phone and told her what was going on and to make sure all the doors were locked.

I sat on a bench and waited. I had been there for about ten minutes or so when I heard the snarling again. There is a security light on a timer mounted outside of the back porch. It was on and shining towards the greenhouse. There is an additional security light by the driveway that comes on if triggered by something moving nearby. I heard some movement near the utility shed again, then another thud and a brief shrieking sound.

Suddenly the security light above the driveway came on. It was a huge winged creature with a long thin tail. It was hideous and looked like it had bat skin and short horns on weird snake-like head. It opened its wings at one point. I say the wingspan was at least eight meters. I didn't notice feathers. It stood about three to four meters high as well. It was snarling and thrashing its head as it ran towards the marsh. I really know of no animal to reference it to.

One of my neighbors came running out, but he didn't see it. As I described what I witnessed, he looked shocked at what I was saying. I don't know if he believed me or not. We decided to call the police and report an unknown animal on the property. I didn't want to describe what I'm sure I saw.

The next day, I contacted a zoologist in Montreal and was referred to a cryptozoologist in Sherbrooke. Neither of them offered much help and neither volunteered to come and *examine the area. The police found nothing, though my yard had four dig marks in it. It looked like someone took a shovel and over-turned the soil.*

I haven't heard any sounds since that incident. If you like to contact me, feel free to do so." MS

I contacted the witness after a few days. I talked to his wife earlier and she stated that she didn't see the creature, but she heard it. The witness told me that the police weren't interested and that they directed him to contact wildlife & animal control. The witness and his wife moved to Magog from western Ontario two years ago. He is not familiar with the outdoors. He didn't offer much more information but refused to give me contact information of his neighbors. He agreed to allow me to post the report.

I will state that I have heard and read strange phenomena associated with the Lake Magog area over the years, especially related to Bigfoot sightings.

LATE 1970S – HARLEM, NEW YORK CITY

THE FOLLOWING account was forwarded to me by the eyewitness in September 2012:

"During the late 1970s, as I and my brother Mark were late and racing to The Jazz Mobile jazz school in Harlem, I saw an unusual spiraling object in the sky. It made such smooth tight circles that it was unnatural on such a windless day.

Though I called Mark's attention to it, he continued to run for we did not have time to stop. Jazz Mobile was a weekend school and its policy was if you were late you were marked absent and two absences you were out. So, he was right in telling me to forget it and come on as he went racing toward the school.

At four o'clock when we were on our way home, I remembered the object and looked for it as we were heading back to the subway. As we neared the lot, I saw the thing was still there and stopped to try and focus in on it. To my shock I saw what I was looking at was a big bird not too far away from us riding the heat thermals. I called Mark's attention to it again and he stopped, and his mouth dropped open. This bird was grayish brown and did not flap its wings like other birds did that I had seen do in the skies over New York. It would just barely move them and soar without doing it again. It was not a seagull, eagle, hawk, osprey, buzzard, or condor. First, I thought it was just a big bird until it started flying through thunder heads, so it was way up there, and not as close to the ground as we first thought it was.

"How could it be so high up but still look so huge?" I asked aloud. "Do you realize how big that thing has to be, when it comes down?" Mark said, his voice tensing up. We better get the hell to the subway."

Where we were standing, we were in an open space for they were renovating the area and most of the old tenements had been torn down. So, we were surrounded by vacant lots and abandoned buildings. Mark was right if that thing got into its mind to come down and grab one of us. There was nothing there to hide under or hold on to. At that moment it flew into a cloud and did not come out of it. We hurried to the subway and went home.

The next weekend as I was getting out of bed a news report came in over NEWS 1010 radio about a man and a woman somewhere upstate New York who had fought off a giant bird that had tried to carry either a child or one of them off. I called the news station with hopes to talk to someone and see if I could get in contact with the couple I had heard about. But I was told that the news I was hearing was on a tape and there was no one for me to talk to in the station. I was told however that the report had come in over the Reuters machine so maybe there is a record of it somewhere in their archives.

I have looked for that report since that day. If obtained, I will be able to pinpoint the year, month and date of my sighting because that happened a week after my sighting. We never returned to the area again. I do not know if it was because of our sighting or not but we did not speak of it." PG

After a few attempts, I was unable to acquire a report described by the eyewitness.

SUMMER 2002 NEAR ROUND LAKE BEACH, IL

I RECEIVED the following report in October 2012 from a witness in Illinois:

"Back in the summer of 2002 during the late morning to early afternoon we were driving south on Highway 83 leaving Round Lake Beach, Illinois going towards Grayslake when we were startled by something large and black crossing in front of the car and landing in small open area of brush to our left. One wing easily filled the entire view ahead of us.

We saw that one huge black bird had landed next to another one and that they were devouring what looked like a small deer or a large dog. It was just for an instant, but they were prehistoric looking and larger than the local turkey buzzards. We watched the evening news thinking that some large vultures may have escaped the zoo, but we saw no mention of any such creatures. We often wondered if anyone else had seen anything like these large black birds in northern Illinois.

Thank you for posting the article and letting me know that I wasn't the only one who saw this." SR

These big black bird sightings have been reported historically throughout Illinois and Indiana. The witness stated this it looked 'prehistoric' but didn't elaborate on the description.

MAY 22, 2013 – NEW KENT, VA

I RECEIVED the following account on May 27, 2013:

"On the 22nd of May, this year, I was driving west on New Kent Highway, just before Rt 106, in Virginia, around 8:30 am. I was driving under the speed limit of forty-five mph and I came around a bend and slowed down more because about thirty yards ahead of the car a huge bird was in the center of the road, straddling the dotted line with its back to me.

New Kent is basically a swamp with islands of high ground. Because of the terrain, housing properties are kind of jammed together on 'high ground' with lots of alternating hill/steep ravine wooded land of the swamp between. We have all kinds of big birds in our area. There are bald eagles, ospreys, herons, turkey vultures, all kinds of hawks, wild turkeys, several kinds of geese, etc. So, seeing a bird in the road is no real surprise.

What made me stop the car twelve feet away from it was the fact the dang thing's head was taller than my hood! I could feel myself starting to grin that grin we do when we just can't believe what we are seeing and suspect a joke. Then it opened its wings. I won't tell you what I said. I was shocked!

I was on a two-lane road with gravel shoulders. This thing's wingtips were touching gravel on both sides! With two slow motion swoops (my window was down, radio off, and I heard its wings pushing the air. It did make a slow "ssshhwooop" sound), it was up and blotting out everything else in my windshield. It then banked left on a wingtip (literally, it was completely vertical with a full view of the whole back of its body) and glided into the woods between the trees. I remember craning my head over the steering wheel and up to see all of it as it banked.

I have no idea how long I sat there in the middle of the road with my mouth open, totally blank, mentally, feeling like I had been slapped silly. The only word that surfaced was 'Thunderbird!' Now, like most American kids, I had heard of Thunderbirds, but honestly, I had never given a single thought as to what they would look like. But that was the word that surfaced. I supposed, if you had asked me before that day, I would have drawn a Micmac totem pole style thing. This was not that.

When I finally cruised past where it had cut through the woods, you can believe I was looking for it. No sign. I immediately called my husband, feeling silly and not mentioning what I thought it was, I asked what bird in Virginia had a fifteen foot wingspan (I wasn't brave enough to tell him it was more like twenty feet). He said none. To his credit, he didn't try to tell me I hadn't seen what I was describing, merely suggested that it may have seemed bigger than it really was due to proximity.

But here's the strange thing. My beloved grandfather was a mountain man, a lifelong hunter and naturalist. He would take us camping my whole childhood, teaching us about wildlife from up close. He taught me how to estimate an *animal's size from surrounding markers. And you can't get more specific than a road-span. So, what did I see?*

It was a dark charcoal color while on the road, but its feathers were a rusty red-brown when it launched into the sunlight. Its tail was a long triangle (with a very slight point on the end/center), like a hawk's. Its wings were just unbelievable. I had a hard time looking at both at the same time. I had to look from one to the other. They weren't shaped like a hawk's, more like a sea gulls, if you can picture it. Its body was torpedo shaped, no neck to speak of and a flat head. Due to the angle, I didn't see it's face or beak and when I could see it bank, I was honestly trying to take in the wings and couldn't tell you anything about the shape of the head in flight. Though, I think if it had a long neck and extended it in flight, I would've noticed. The impression I got of the legs were 'short and stubby.' I didn't see the feet.

I've been trying to talk myself out of having seen it since that day. I didn't try to look it up, because that would make it 'real.' Does that make sense? Tonight, I finally decided to try a search online. Every description of 'modern' Thunderbird sighting is comparable to what I saw. Go ahead and laugh. I don't blame you. You weren't there. A week ago, I would have done the same." SM

DECEMBER 15, 2015 - NEAR NEW KENT COUNTY AIRPORT, VA

Two-and-a-half years later, I receive a telephone call from another witness from the same general area. I asked the witness to write the account and forward to me:

"On Monday Dec 15th at 6:45 pm I was traveling on Airport Rd near the New Kent Co. Airport. This section of road went by the New Kent trash collection center. The road is bordered by woods on both sides.

As I approached this location, I noticed something large and dark on the road very near the trash collection lot. I hit my brakes and came within fifty feet of what appeared to be a huge bird. Like I told you on the telephone, when I say huge, I mean something of unbelievable size. It had the overall shape of an eagle. It also had talons which were lighter in color. The beak seemed too large and long for its face. The overall color was black. The height was at least eight feet, probably more as it bobbed up and down. It may have been eating something when I approached it.

Its head moved toward the direction of my car and made a grunting sound. It turned away from me and the long tail with feathers swung around in my direction. The wings, which extended across the road, unfurled as it lifted off the surface. The wings were massive, but like I said reached past the width of the road. I told you twenty-five feet on the telephone. I still believe that is a correct estimate.

I searched 'monster birds' and found your telephone number and email. I looked at different images of eagles and hawks online but there was nothing that closely resembled this bird. Thanks for talking to me." JD

After I finished talking to JD, I went to Google Maps in order to find the location. I then realized that it was within a few miles of a large bird sighting in May 2013. The descriptions were different in most respects, but both were of birds of enormous size. The entire area seems to have a lot of wetlands & swamps.

During our phone conversation, JD mentioned that the bird

had something in its talons. He said he got a brief look as it started to fly away but mentioned that the 'legs were dangling from one side.'

I brought up the subject of pterosaurs to JD, but he said it absolutely had feathers. Could this have been a Thunderbird? I was somewhat taken aback by the size description of eight feet high and wingspan of twenty-five feet. This is bigger than any other Thunderbird-type sighting I've ever received.

JULY 26, 2015 – PINCHOT LAKE NEAR DILLSBURG, PA

I RECEIVED a telephone call from a young man name Bill who lives near Dillsburg, PA. He had second-hand information concerning a 'weird large bird' that was seen flying near the Pinchot Lake dam. He stated that the sighting was made Sunday, July 26 around 8:45 PM while the witness was on Conley Rd. The witness is a York County employee who is Bill's relative through marriage.

The 'bird' was flying south toward Alpine Rd. about one hundred and twenty-five feet above the ground. The witness observed the cryptid for approximately fifteen-seconds. He estimated that the total body length was five to six feet with a very wide wingspan. The wings were described as 'bat-like' and there was a distinctive oval-shaped head. He also stated that it seemed to glide as opposed to its wings flapping. The features and overall color were dark.

Bill also told me that he had heard of a large bird sighting at the same State Park (Gifford Pinchot SP) several years ago. That is the extent of the information that he could provide to me.

I asked Bill to try and persuade the witness to contact me, but that seems to be a long shot. The witness is apparently quite shaken by the sighting and only disclosed his experience to Bill after some prodding.

As to what this cryptid was is anybody's guess, though I will say that the Pinchot Lake dam is about a quarter mile north of Conewago Creek. I'm not saying that this was another Conewago Phantom sighting, but the location is interesting.

I looked through my archives / media reports and failed to find any similar beings and encounters at the location. I'm leaning to the side of cryptid bird as opposed to a winged humanoid.

LATE 1980S IN CHATTANOOGA, TN

THE FOLLOWING account was forward to me by my colleague Jamie Brian. I sent it along to a local investigator after I completed some research:

"I grew up in Chattanooga, Tennessee and right behind my grandmother's house there was a cemetery. Behind that were railroad tracks. Behind that was some government property that everybody always called 'the TNT.' I was told that the military tested bombs, ammunition, tanks and other stuff back there during World War II.

When we were kids, we would walk back in there, just wasting time in the woods. It was 8000 acres of rolling hills up and down, all over the place.

I was back there with my friend one day. I was maybe 13 or 14 years old. We kept thinking we were seeing someone following us. We couldn't really make out any definition, but it just looked like there was a white figure on top of the hill every time we'd get down to the bottom of the hill. We'd get down to this little plateau and we had three ways we could take. We could go back towards the house and we could go left or right and deeper into the woods. One of the ways went up a hill.

Sudden, I hear my friend say, 'Hey, what's that!?' I look up in the tree and there is this gigantic bird sitting on the top branches. Before I could even turn up and look at it, I hear this giant whooshing sound behind us and whatever this was, it was following us. It took flight and landed right next to the other one in the tree and when it did, it broke the tree limb. The limbs came crashing down, with a big loud sound. Both took off into the air, wingspan larger than I ever want to imagine at this point. These birds were big enough to carry off a human being. You could surely hear it. I mean, it was like a whoosh! After they flew off, we quickly skedaddled home.

That was the last time I went back into those woods. A Volkswagen plant was built there not long after our incident." M

This immense tract of land, where this sighting occurred, is part of what used to be the Volunteer Army Ammunition Plant; known locally as VAAP. Consisting of over 7,000 acres located in the heart of the county, the area had always been closed to the public and heavily guarded. Because of this, the area holds a certain mystique for residents.

VAAP's history stretches to World War II when the federal government acquired 7,000 acres for TNT production. Employment peaked at about 3,500 workers and production ebbed and waned over the years with the ammunition demands for the Korean and Vietnam wars. Production ceased at the facility in 1977.

Is there some type of connection between ordinance plants and winged cryptids? The Point Pleasant Mothman was seen at the West Virginia Ordinance Works on numerous occasions.

JULY 2011 NEAR MANITOU FALLS, ONTARIO, CANADA

I RECEIVED the following account on July 30, 2018:

"Sir - I heard you on 'Paranormal Horizon' radio last night and tried to call-in but the show was ending. You were talking about inter-dimensional creatures. I believe I saw something that may fit that bill.

In July 2011 my wife and I were spending a weekend at a friend's cabin, about fifteen kilometers north of Manitou Falls, Ontario, Canada. We were both sitting on the porch looking into the woods. There were two spotlights shining off the porch, so the woods and the open area in front of the cabin were well-lit. I had spent a lot of time in this general area as a boy, and I was aware of the wildlife that lived there.

It was close to midnight, as we sat and talked. It was a very mild still night, but for some reason the usual sounds of the woods were subdued. I wasn't alarmed, but it did seem strange. Sometimes when a Lynx hunts at night, things do quiet down; so, I assumed that may be what was going on. I kept my eyes open just in case another predator was about. Eventually my wife wanted to go inside, so I obliged her and followed. I left the porch spotlights on. We went to bed around 1:30 am and both of us quickly dozed off.

The next thing I remember is my wife shaking me, telling me to wake up. She said she had heard a 'scream' coming from the front of the cabin. She wasn't used to being in the outdoors, so I told her it was either an Owl or Lynx. She insisted that no animal could have made that terrible noise; that it sounded like a woman was in distress. I looked at my phone. It was 2:33 am. I got out of bed and walked into the front living room. I looked out the window but didn't see anything.

She was right behind me. Then the scream pierced the night again. This time I heard it, and it wasn't like anything I've ever heard before. We stood by the cabin window and watched the woods. About

10 *minutes later, we heard something on top of the cabin porch roof. It sounded like it was jumping up and down. It was so loud and forceful, I thought it may go through the porch roof. We continued to watch, when suddenly, this huge winged creature jettisoned from above towards the woods. It was massive and dark in color. The wings were fully open and not moving; like it was gliding towards the trees. We caught a decent look of this creature as it sailed upwards into the dark sky, then descended back towards the edge of the woods. It performed this maneuver two more times, until it came streaming, and screaming, towards the open ground in front of the cabin; and then it vanished! The wings had been tight against the body and it looked like a dark missile about to slam into the clearing but disappeared before it hit the ground!*

We both jumped and let out a huge gasp. It was the most shocking experience I had ever had. My wife was wide-eyed and had to sit down. What in the world was that thing?

I have tried to comprehend what we witnessed that night, and I still have no idea as to what it was. It had arms and legs, but the body was scrawny and flexible. It's hard to describe. The head was barely visible. Overall, I'd guess it was four feet or so in height and the wide billowy wings spread out to at least fifteen feet when fully extended. The scream was the most memorable part of this experience. It really did sound like a frightened woman, but the decibel level made our ears uncomfortable.

A few days later, I asked my friend if he had ever seen anything unusual at the cabin. The most exciting event he could recall was a Badger getting into the kitchen one night.

That was the extent of it. I decided not to go into details with him but did say that my wife and I had an eerie night and that we didn't get much sleep because of strange noises coming from the woods. He just shrugged his shoulders and said nothing.

Do you believe that this flying creature disappeared into another reality, as you mentioned on the show? I appreciate your thoughts." JK

I talked to 'JK' by telephone. He currently lives in North Dakota. His encounter left a lot of questions. He was positive that this was a corporeal creature and that both he and his wife were not hallucinating. In some respect, it resembles the activity of a winged humanoid, but I believe that this was a type of cryptid bird. As far as the entity vanishing, I don't discount the witness account since I have been told similar scenarios in the past.

JULY 6, 2018 NEAR CONSECON, ONTARIO, CANADA

I RECEIVED the following account the day after the incident:

"On Friday, July 6, 2018, a friend and I were driving out to Pleasant Bay, a small beach area outside of Consecon, Ontario. It was around 8:30 pm and the sun was only just beginning to set on the horizon. We figured we still had a good ninety minutes before it got dark, so we got some McDonald's coffee and headed out. The beach is way out in the middle of nowhere, down a lengthy stretch of highway with lots of trees lining both sides of the road and broken up by the occasional farmer's field.

About ten minutes outside of Consecon, while cruising on the Loyalist Parkway, I noticed something in the trees just as we approached a bend in the road. We were moving quite fast, but something caught my eye. A fleeting glimpse of what looked like grayish legs (talons?) making a ruckus in the trees on the left side of the road. I didn't get much of a look at it but my friend, who was behind the wheel, certainly did. As we zoomed by, he craned his neck out the window, trying to get a look at whatever it was. He eventually turned back to me, blurting, "Holy shit, did you see that bird? That was the biggest frigging bird I've ever seen!"

In his usual expletive filled way, he indicated that the bird he saw had a 'massive' wingspan, was brownish in color, and was as big or bigger than the car slightly ahead of us on the road. When I asked him what it was doing, he told me that it was trying to jump from one branch to another branch, with some difficulty. It was so big that the branches could not bear its weight. I wonder if it was looking for roadkill and the passing cars (us and the car ahead of us) maybe spooked it.

My friend is accustomed to seeing Turkey Vultures and other large birds as he often accompanies his father back north on hunting trips, but this was bigger than anything he had ever seen before. Concerning why we didn't turn around to get a picture or get a better look, it just honestly didn't occur to us. It was just something odd that we passed on the road and we wanted to get to the beach and have a swim before it got too dark.

It should be noted that my friend has not even a remote interest in the paranormal or cryptozoology as he feels it's all a bunch of foolishness. He is completely oblivious to all the recent giant bird & winged humanoid sightings being reported around the world, so I found it funny that he was the one who saw it."

The names of the witnesses are being withheld. I found this account to be very interesting since there have been several winged humanoid sightings throughout Ontario, Quebec and the Niagara region of New York over the past two years. The description seemed to indicate that this was a large cryptid bird.

NO DATE – NOLANVILLE, TX

On February 2, 2019, I received the following account:

"A few years ago, when I lived in Nolanville, Texas, I was taking a back road to work. As I slowed for a curve that veered to my left, I was doing about twenty-five or thirty miles per hour. The sun was just coming over the mesquite tree tops. I was heading north about one hundred yards from the curve. Suddenly something moved to my right in the knee-high weeds. I glanced over to see if it were a calf or some other animal. It suddenly spread its wings and flew right over my Mitsubishi Mirage going from the passenger side over to the left of the road. Its wings would have covered my whole car. It was grey speckled and had a long beak. If it would have flown over me much lower, it would have scraped the top of my car with its feet, which were huge. I gasped and said aloud, "What in the world was that?"

I continued to drive to work and after I got home, I told my daughter about it. She said she had seen the same thing just a few days earlier in the same spot. She said it flew right in front of her but was higher up and flew over her car. She tried to watch it in her rearview mirror, but lost sight of it. She said she was going to tell me about it, but it slipped her mind. We would watch for it after that, but we never saw it again.

The wingspan was about ten feet. Its body size was

comparable to a large dog. I didn't see its neck enough to determine if it were long or not. It did had feathers." DC

MAY 5, 2019 – PA STATE GAME LAND 180

I received the following account on May 31, 2019:

"Hi Lon. This sighting happened this past Friday, May 24, 2019 of Memorial Day Weekend. It was around noon, and my family and I were driving to our extended family's lake house on Lake Wallenpaupack in Pennsylvania. It was a sunny, clear day and we were heading west along Highway 6. This long stretch is heavily wooded and rural on both sides, and at that instance we were driving through State Game Lands Number 180.

I was driving so my eyes were fixed upon the road ahead. There was another car roughly fifty feet in front of us. Then, from the left side of the road, I saw something emerge from the treetops and fly across the road right in front of the other car, so I would say it was about sixty to seventy feet from my point of view. I got a very good look at it as it crossed in the air, and it had all the features of a bird, except this animal was gigantic. I'm aware and have seen all the different types of birds in the area, the largest ones being bald eagles, hawks, and vultures. I'm also very familiar with all the different types of water birds (this did not resemble a water bird whatsoever). The profile of the flying animal was longer than the car in front of me was wide, which was at minimum six feet. The other car quickly braked as it flew past them obviously astonished by the sight as well. The animal flew over the road and disappeared into the thick forest on the right side of the road.

My wife, who was in the passenger seat, saw it clearly as well and said aloud, 'Wow, what's that?!' What we saw was evidently a bird, but an unusually massive one." K

SUMMER 2017 – LIHI, UT

I received a telephone call, on July 2, 2019, from an eyewitness 'JR' who claims she observed a huge winged creature in Lihi, Utah.

This incident occurred in the summer of 2017, on a very hot clear day at approximately midday. JR states that she had stopped for a traffic light when she noticed several Sandhill Cranes flying across the sky in front of her. She says that she was about 150-200 feet away. Apparently, this is a nesting area for Sandhill Cranes.

As she watched, she saw a large dark wing creature descending towards the cranes. As it got closer, she was astonished by the size. It was avian in form, with feathered wings that she estimates spanned 20 feet are more. JR has a Biology degree and is well-versed in the local avian wildlife.

The monstrous bird literally snatched one of the Sandhill Cranes and ascended on a thermal. It quickly headed off and away from the area. JR said that she noticed a band of white color on the front edge of the wings. She likened the shape to that of a Golden Eagle, but that the body was smaller in comparison to the huge wings. She also said the massive bird was 'at least' four times the size of the Sandhill Cranes.

JR said that she noticed only one other car at the intersection and doubts that they witnessed the event. She contacted her professor and asked for his opinion. He was flummoxed and told JR that she must have misidentified the bird. She is positive at what she saw. JR has made many attempts to identify the cryptid bird but has been frustrated. She found me on Google and called to retell her observation.

SUMMER 2008 – KENNEDY LAKE, VANCOUVER ISLAND, BC

I RECEIVED the following email on October 14, 2019:

"In the summer of 2008, my brother and I were returning home from Kennedy Lake (Vancouver Island, BC) on a logging road. I noticed something massive flying overhead. Surprised, I pointed it out to my brother also (passenger seat). We both watched this thing fly ahead of us for a minute or two. It flew like a bat, but was MASSIVE. My brother and I are certain of what we saw and it still sticks with us to this day. Any similar sightings? Let me know if you have more questions." RP

I called RP and received more information. RP and his brother were driving home along a wide logging road near Kennedy Lake on Vancouver Island, BC. Suddenly, at approximately 5 pm local time, a huge bat-winged being flew over the car and maintained flight about thirty feet in front of them. RP sped up in order to stay near the winged anomaly. They were able to watch it for thirty seconds to one-minute and got an excellent view.

RP's described the entity as resembling a monstrous bat-like creature. The wings were like that of a bat or mythical gargoyle and it flew in the same manner as a bat, but at a much slower flapping rate. The wing span was almost as wide as the road, at least ten feet. It was all black in color. The body was long and thin. They never got a very good look at the head. The legs were very long and tapered, extending behind the flying being.

They were both shocked at what they were observing. RP, his brother and family were very familiar with the outdoors, particularly the fauna of Vancouver Island. RP stated that he searched online for an idea of what they saw, and stumbled upon my contact information. He felt comfortable enough to share his information with me.

9

THE SOUTHWEST FLORIDA GARGOYLES

In September 2017, I began to receive reports of gargoyle-like winged humanoids in southwest Florida, particularly in Pasco County and other locations just east of Tampa. During this time period, the team had already been investigating the Chicago winged humanoid phenomenon for almost 6 months. The comparisons between the Florida and Chicagoland beings were similar, but a few differences did exist.

One of these differences was that the Florida winged humanoids seemed to be hunting the local whitetail deer and in two instances, several carcasses were noticed by the witnesses. The Chicago area winged humanoids were never seen with any prey. There were no reports of missing / dead pets or small animals connected with these beings either. I did receive a report from a witness in northwest Indiana who claimed that they observed a winged humanoid catching fish in a local marshland, but that was never corroborated.

EARLY SEPTEMBER 2017 NEAR ZEPHYRHILLS, FL

I RECEIVED the following account on September 22, 2017. I was able to talk to the witness the same day:

> "Hello. I had read about these encounters of bat-like humanoids and obviously thought it was pretty fascinating. I just recently started a new job in Clearwater, Florida where I'm delivering donuts for a major company. I deliver along a route which consists of four different stops. I drive from Clearwater to Port Richey, then to Brooksville and Zephyrhills.
>
> Two weeks ago I had the night off, so another guy worked my route. And in case you don't know Brooksville, Fl and Zephyrhills, Fl., both are riddled with dark roads with no street lights, and just trees to the left and right side of the road.
>
> While he was driving between his third and fourth stop near Zephyrhills, (on Rt 98 / US 301 at about 3:30 am) he said he saw this 'thing' floating stationary about fifteen feet off the ground next to a tree. As he got closer he realized it looked like a dark-colored humanoid in a cannonball position just floating in the air. Like frozen. He said by the time he got over the initial shock of seeing this creature, it unraveled itself and spread out its legs and giant bat-like wings. He didn't know what color the creature was but he said it was a dark color or black and it had human-like legs. And he said at the same moment it spread its wings and legs it flew toward his truck at an unrealistic speed. He said he almost crashed the truck in the ditch because it basically paralyzed him with fear. He said it happened so fast he didn't get a look at the face but he said it was probably between five and six feet tall and dark colored and it had human legs with bat wings.
>
> He also said that about a half mile before he saw the creature he saw a bunch of dead deer on the side of the road. Like piles of deer, two separate piles of at least four deer. He

assumes it was eating them. The witness is a pretty soft-spoken dude and intelligent. The way he tells the story, I can tell it really freaked him out." AP

I called AP, who recounted the incident that the witness described to him. He told me that the witness told him that the being looked like a 'skinny gargoyle.' He was unable to get a good look at the face, so there was no mention of red eyes or other facial features. The legs were definitely human-like and the wings span was at least twelve or more feet in width. AP also stated that while explaining the encounter, the witness started to look pale and distressed. AP told me that he has his camera ready with him at all times and plans to keep his eyes open while driving along that route.

A few weeks later, on October 6, 2017, AP contacted me by email:

"Hey Lon. This is AP. I spoke to you on the phone a couple weeks ago about how one of the drivers on my route saw the winged creature in Zephyrhills, Florida. Well, I wanted to update you and tell you that I was off of work a couple nights ago and the guy who covered my shift, a different driver from the original email I sent you, also saw the creature. He texted me early in the morning and told me he was a believer now because he also saw the thing.

His description was that it was tall, like six feet or so. He said it was dark gray and he also said that it had a wide wing span. Its body was very skinny and in segments like an ant. Thorax, abdomen, etc. He said it flew over the road from right to left. He said it flew so fast that it was hard to really make out what it actually looked like. It was in the same area of the previous sighting as well. But instead of on Rt. 98 it was on

US 301 which is a road that 98 leads to. US 301 is a much longer and a darker road than Rt. 98. He also said that there were deer everywhere. So I'm starting to think that this thing eats deer.

I'm driving out there right now, so if I see anything I will obviously update you again." AP

I later talked to AP by telephone. He had not seen the winged humanoid, but he has seen deer skeletons and hides at several points along Rt. 98 and US 301.

EARLY FEBRUARY 2018 – ZEPHYRHILLS, FL

ON SATURDAY, February 3, 2018, at 3:14 pm ET I received a telephone call from a witness in Zephyrhills, Florida (Pasco County) in reference to a recent encounter / sighting of a winged being at their residence. After listening to the information, I asked the witness to write down what they experienced and to forward to me. I soon received the following account:

"I called you from Zephyrhills, Florida on Saturday. I explained to you that my sister and son have been experiencing some strange phenomenon. I explained to you that we weren't sure whether it had a demonic origin, spiritual in some way, or what in the world it could be?

We had cleansed the house in the spiritual sense with Holy Oil and prayer. This had not worked.

It started with scratching noises in the walls, along with heavy human-like steps on our roof right before or after. The steps were fast. There was fluttering noises of wings of a sort. We noticed that there was a large cement block on the bottom of the house moved out, no longer sealed tight as usual.

We somehow packed this in a file in our minds, in order to deal with ordinary life on life's terms. However, the enormous wings on this other new creature we have witnessed has really taken us to a different chapter in life.

We had those noises of scratching on the walls, fluttering of wings, and human-like steps on our roof, and finally we eye-witnessed the strange phenomenon. My son yelled for me while in the bathroom. He said, "please, come now, it is right out the window!" I ran and looked out the locked window. There were noises coming from below the window, like it came out and stretched up. I saw blackish darkness almost cover the entire window. It was part of a wing. A very small part. I say this because it hovered up quickly with two enormous wings, at about five feet each. I only saw the back of its head which was blackish in color. It went ever so quickly in the air, away from the house, and gone. What the heck is this?

We started researching about it, Lon. This is when we found information on you. We saved your phone contact, and called. Please notify me of anything you may find out in your other areas if it pertains to this.

Should we be fearful of our lives, or our cat? Thank you for speaking to me, and for letting me know we could call you if we need to." DS

The information provided by the witness in the email is very close to what we originally discussed. The sheer fear expressed on the telephone was evident. I asked a seasoned investigator, who lives nearby, to contact the witness and make arrangements for an on-site interview. The interview did occur, but not further evidence was collected. The two previous sightings of a winged being (described as a gargoyle) occurred just a few miles north of this location.

JANUARY 2018 – BRANDON, FL

I RECEIVED the following information was forwarded to me by my associate Jamie Brian on June 2, 2018. It was a response to the video that Jamie produced regarding the southwest Florida gargoyle incidents:

> *"You won't believe me but I live in Florida, and about 6 months ago on the way to work early in the morning, I swear I saw a gargoyle in the Brandon, FL area, not too far from Zephyrhills. I literally only clicked this video hoping you were talking about Florida."* S

I asked my Jamie, who is the administrator of the YouTube channel, if he could contact the witness for further information. He received the following information:

> *"Not too much to add. I was on my way to work. It was about 6:40 am and quite a few months ago. It was very dark out, very still as I approached an intersection. It was a red light, so I stopped and was about three cars back. When the light turned green, I looked up and off in the distance there was a human-sized gargoyle looking thing flying across the sky. I'd say probably two to three hundred feet up and a good distance away. It was pretty quick but it flew behind some trees and a building so I lost sight of it. I was in so much awe of what I was looking at, I couldn't even muster out a single word to get the guy in the truck with me to look up at it."* S

I realize that there isn't much detail, but the area is approximately fifteen to twenty miles south of the three previous sightings of a similarly described winged being.

EARLY DECEMBER 2019 – TAMPA, FL

I RECEIVED the following account just a few days after the sighting:

> "I had an incident in Tampa, Florida; a winged creature sighting. Driving to work early in the morning. It wasn't dark but not quite daylight. Driving around a curve on a road where I know I'm approaching a light (it's always red and I always have to stop). For one of the only times I can remember I somehow was the first vehicle stopped at the intersection. I knew I needed to keep an eye on the light, so I'm looking up waiting for it to turn green.
>
> At that moment, I just happened to catch sight of something moving along to my left. It was flying from left to right (south to north). I won't lie, I did not get to see it for long but in that one to three-seconds it was as clear as I could possibly of imagined. It looked just like a gargoyle. Large bat-like wings, hands crutched up tight in front, legs kind of pulled up along the body as well. It was gliding along. The wings never flapped.
>
> Now I don't claim to have the world's greatest eye or am I an expert on all things relating to distance, but I know what it looked like. I'm certain of its size, which would be about the size of a large man, and I know it wasn't that far in front of me. I had a lot of objects in my fore view to help get a good perception. Could it have been anything else other than a gargoyle? Of course. I'm not crazy. That's just what it looked like." SS

Southwest Florida is well-known for a high number of unexplained activity. UFO encounters, Skunk Ape sightings and occasional alien being incidents have been reported and documented regularly in this part of Florida. The fact that people are reporting winged humanoids, in particular gargoyles, in southwest Florida is not too surprising.

10

'MANTA RAY' SHAPED FLYING CRYPTIDS

DECEMBER 3, 2004 NEAR ASHTON, WV

In September 2010, I had written an article in reference to the strange phenomena that regularly occurred in Pt. Pleasant, WV and the surrounding area. As a result of that article, I received a very interesting response and further communication. This was the first, of many, sightings of this elusive flying cryptid:

"Hi Lon, thanks for responding so quickly. Here are my drawings and report:

Date: Dec. 3, 2004 Time:6:00 - 7:00 pm
    Weather Conditions: clear and already dark. Moon hadn't risen yet

Location: Traveling south on Rt.2 in WV from Point Pleasant to Huntington WV. Near Ashton WV

A friend and I were traveling on Rt. 2 towards Huntington WV. I was on my way to set up my booth for an art show and my mind was occupied with the booth set up and show logistics. We had just gone over the railroad tracks outside of Ashton WV and were on a long straight stretch of road. There was distant oncoming traffic and the headlights were on. There were no cars behind us in sight. I was in the passenger seat and my friend was driving. I noticed a sudden movement in the sky over the Ohio River to my right in front of the car. It was a grayish, smooth, winged shape. the shape swooped in a figure 8 in front of the windshield and then was suddenly gone to the left of us. It didn't fly out of sight, it was just gone. This happened very quickly, but as I am a visual artist, it was impressed into my memory banks!

Size: Bigger than the car. The wingspread was wider than the two lane road we were on. The wings seemed to stretch wider somehow as it did the figure 8 swoop. It was never more than 25 feet away from us as it flew towards the windshield. We thought it was going to crash into the windshield! At one point during the swoop it was only about 5 feet off of the pavement.

Color: Grey, translucent like a jellyfish. As it banked and swooped I could see many angles of it and somehow it looked more transparent as it turned some parts to us. I immediately thought it was like a manta ray. The body was flattish like a manta ray or a bat. The wings were long and smooth and sort of pointed at the tip. I saw no texture or roughness on it, only smooth surface.

Characteristics: Only body and wings-no head, eyes, tail, or feet. It did not look humanoid in any way. On the other hand, it wasn't a bird either. It moved more like something in the ocean would move. It did not flap the wings like a bird, or flutter them like a bat, but stretched them instead. My friend (who alas passed away a year ago) said to him the wings looked ragged like there were pieces coming off of them.

He also said he got a good look at the underneath and it looked grey and smooth. This absolutely was not a machine! It was articulated like a living creature and seemed like something organic. As I look back on this sighting, I wonder if it was something playing with us - It happened so quickly that the only scary part was when we thought it was going to crash into the windshield. It was so beautiful and strange! It reminded me of a sea creature more than anything else, maybe our air is like water to them.

The only other time in my life I have ever seen anything remotely similar was in 2000 in Clay Co. WV, driving along a one lane road along the Elk River (a river was present in both instance-I just realized) In that case, I was alone and for about a mile as I drove, I kept noticing a shimmer in front of the car about fifteen feet ahead of the car. This was late morning in the summer. It preceded the car at the same distance for several minutes, then I noticed a shadow on the road too, large and shaped sort of like a bird. I looked up out of the windshield and there was a large crow flying above me. But what I first saw in front of the car was not a shadow, it was a disturbance in the air in front of my car that looked like a heat mirage sort of but was very close. This was a curvy country road right by the river. I had never seen heat mirages on that road before or since. At the time I thought that it was just sort of weird, then very close to that time I had a very lucid dream that I was in my car flying over the river right near the place where I saw the shadow.

As an artist, my mind is open to many possibilities and explanations. I think the unseen world is just a small vibrational frequency away. As a child I was fascinated by *fairies and nature spirits and spent a lot of time alone outdoors." Name Withheld*

This particular sighting and description is unique and most likely represents an unclassified or non-terrestrial entity. The area along the Ohio River (southern Ohio and southwest West Virginia) has had a large number of other paranormal events including UFOs, large apparitions and hauntings, native and folklore based creatures, etc.

JULY 2006 – HAMPTON BAYS, NY

I RECEIVED A VERY interesting email on 12/3/2011, that described an encounter with a 'manta ray' shaped flying entity on Long Island:

Date of Event: July, 2006

Time: 9:00 - 10:00 pm EST (estimated time frame)

Weather Conditions: Clear, bright night. The moon was very bright and large and you could see every star as the further east you go, the less light pollution you experience

Location: Traveling West on Dune Road, stopped at the Jetty in Hampton Bays, NY (the end of Dune Road)

"My experience occurred sometime in July 2006, right after my father had passed away. I regularly take long drives out to the East end of Long Island and walk on the beaches at night as it's very peaceful and isolated. The beach in Hampton Bays (the Jetty at the end of Dune Road) is particularly nice at

night. I've been there at least a hundred times and had never experienced anything out of the ordinary. I took my then-fiancee out there to show him the phosphorescent shrimp that wash ashore as he had never seen them; we parked the car and proceeded to walk down to the water. The moon was very bright that night, so you could look down the long stretch of beach and see everything. We were alone. No other people were on the beach, no other cars were parked nearby and all establishments were closed; it's a rather remote area aside from a few scattered private residences and a few restaurant/bars. Now, a bit about me: I'm an artist, was raised with an open mind, I'm a healthy skeptic and I don't scare easily.

As soon as we stepped onto the beach I had a feeling of general unease; that instinctive fear that one would experience in the presence of a predator. I chose to ignore it; occasionally peeking over my shoulder at the long, empty stretch of beach behind me but mostly focusing on the tiny glowing shrimp beneath our feet. At one point I felt a presence and again, chose to ignore it as I've dealt with that quite a bit in my thirty years. I had not voiced my unease to my fiancee, so he was completely unaware. About five to ten minutes into our short walk we were both hunched over, his back facing the jetty, mine facing the stretch of empty beach when he started peering over my shoulder, up into the sky. Perplexed, he'd look for a second, then look away. At this point I was still trying to retain my composure and not look. Finally, after a few minutes, he looked over my head and yelled "oh my God! What *is* that?!" I turned to look and 'flying' directly over my head was this huge creature I'd never seen! I will detail as best I can.

It appeared translucent/transparent; no color whatsoever, no visible structure outside of the motion which indicated what it looked like; now, I myself am a visual artist, so this left a very distinct impression on me. This 'creature' was shaped and moving in the way a Manta Ray would; yet completely transparent! No color at all; I could see the stars through this thing; the only thing to allow the structure any appearance was the moonlight shining somehow on its' exterior! It was larger than a standard sedan. Its wingspan was at least, from what I could estimate, ten feet in width; while it was flying, its wings moving up and down. The movement seemed familiar, like that of a gull swooping down and hovering over the shoreline. It was approximately ten to fifteen feet over my head; it had no visible 'head' or 'tail'; no discernible limbs or appendages of any kind. It appeared and moved exactly as a Manta Ray without the 'Cephalic Lobes' or 'tail'. I was completely awe-struck, but that fear took over and after about thirty-seconds of staring at this thing we both turned and bolted toward the car. While running, we both simultaneously jerked our heads to the right in response to a glowing green light which seemed to flash twice (it was not the light from the tower on the jetty, nor was it from any boat; that water was clear). I never looked behind me. We started heading back on Dune Road when we saw what I could only describe as two, smaller 'rays' which moved more like a bat would, flying together from right to left overhead past the car. These two were translucent and had a grayish color to them. Quite strange. They were flying in the direction of the beach, where the larger, more transparent creature was. On the ride home, we spoke about how confused we were, but didn't compare notes on what we had seen. I told him I wanted to wait until we got home to do that.

Now I consider myself a well-educated believer in supernatural/paranormal phenomenon and have a long-standing fascination with cryptids but I always approach everything with a healthy dose of skepticism. As soon as we arrived home, I tore two pages out of a sketchbook, grabbed two pencils and gave one of each to my fiancee, instructed him to draw exactly what he had seen and left the room; I did the same. When we were done, we placed our sketches side by side and they were identical. That was enough confirmation for me. I immediately went online to try to research any reports which would help explain what we had witnessed, but I couldn't find anything at all! It was extremely frustrating. I did report the sighting to the National UFO Reporting Center, but still, until I stumbled across your post, was at a loss for any confirmation or additional reports of this type of creature.

I really would love to hear of anyone else who may have experienced something similar on the East end of Long Island.

Feel free to post this if you like. I'd love some answers as I'm fascinated by this event. It's so difficult to describe the appearance due to the fact that it was transparent, yet we could see the motion. Almost like when heat rises from asphalt and wrinkles the air. I really was amazed and have no idea what this thing could be!

It was so beautiful and strange! It reminded me of a sea creature more than anything else. Maybe our air is like water to them. I feel the same way; I instantly felt that it seemed to be 'swimming' through the air. I also believe that it's possible that multiple dimensions are simply a vibration away; that many things are likely coming over and going back from time to time." Jeni

I was never able to find another sighting on Long Island, NY, but the phenomenon continued to be reported.

JANUARY 25, 2012 – HEBRON, KY

I RECEIVED the following account not long after the actual incident occurred:

"I am a college sophomore who lives in Hebron, Kentucky very close to the Ohio River. On January 25, 2012, around 9:00 pm I was in the car (my mom was driving) going home. It was dark and we were driving like normal. Then she stepped on the brake because a white stingray flying creature about one to two feet across swooped down and flew about four or five feet in front of the car about five feet off the ground. Two cars driving in the opposite direction also hit the brakes for it.

Right after we saw it I thought it looked very strange but I thought I was just over exaggerating until my mom seemed to be startled by its weird stingray appearance. I then got the idea it might have been something different. It definitely was not a bird because it didn't really flap its wings. It looked like it was swimming underwater. Plus, it didn't seem to have a head from my perspective! I looked up what it could possibly be and found your reports of the exact same thing (only bigger) recently. The similarities are astonishing." Name Withheld

FEBRUARY 21, 2012 – LYNCHBURG, VA

I received the following account on the same day of the sighting:

"On February 21, 2012, I was driving home after a workout and some grocery shopping. I was driving on Highway 460 east in Lynchburg, VA when something flew in front of my car, swooped upwards and then was gone. I actually asked myself, "was that a freaking sting ray?" It was smooth, white and about three feet wide, maybe wider. It was the strangest thing I have ever seen in my life. I am not a believer in aliens, paranormal, etc., but I know I saw something, and it wasn't normal at all. I wonder how many other people have seen this creature." MEF

I asked the witness for more details, then received the following:

"It was between Lynchburg, Virginia and Concord, Virginia, approximately one tenth of a mile from Falwell Airport. You can search for Falwell Airport, Lynchburg, VA on Google Maps. There is a small patch of trees between the airport and a small plaza. This is where I saw it.

This creature was solid white, and as I said, about three feet wide, but may have been wider. There were no feathers to suggest it was a bird. I was trying to find owls online that have this similarity, but couldn't find any. There was no head and was very smooth, unlike a sting ray. I did not notice a tail/stinger. It swooped down in front of my car and then up over the windshield and disappeared into the night. It was approximately 9:15 pm EST.

I looked for it coming home today and didn't see it! It was the strangest thing I have ever seen in my life!" MEF

SUMMER 2013 – JORDAN, MN

I received the following report the next day after the encounter:

"Hello - I just saw something I've never seen before. I was just coming home from work. It was about 3:40 am driving through a small town in MN named Jordan. While driving about thirty miles per hour a white stingray type animal flying about five feet off the ground maybe six feet in front of my car swooping through the air almost like swimming. It was not flying very fast so I got a pretty good look at it.

It was dirty white with patches of gray. I only had the lights from my car so color was hard to tell. It was four to five feet in width and about two to three feet in length. It's stomach bulged out about two feet and I could not see any distinct head but I could hardly take my eyes off the wings. I've been all over the country and seen many species of wildlife and NEVER seen anything like this in the air. I have raised river stingrays and have spent hours watching them. It looked like a frigging flying ray! I'm still flipping out.

If you have any questions or have anything to tell me about this creature please get back to me. I feel blessed to see something I had no idea existed. And if you have any pics of this being I would love to see some to be able to compare what I saw. Thanks for the site - I've be up trying to locate this all night.

By the way I forgot to mention it had no feathers but looked like it had a very light coating of fur, like a short haired dog. So I hope this helps you. By the way I have never seen your site up until this point. It is eerie how closely related the stories on your site are to what I saw. I'm almost shivering. Thanks again." J

I called the witness and confirmed much of what he stated in the email.

FEBRUARY 26, 2013 – LAREDO, TX

I RECEIVED the following report after the witness searched the internet for similar sightings:

"I was driving home to my house at 1:20 pm when I came across this stingray grayish-white looking thing flying over my car. It was coming from the lake we have here in Laredo, Texas, heading into the golf course next to it. It was roughly three feet wide, maybe bigger and it had a glide to it. It literally looked like a stingray. It passed about thirty feet in front of me and I watched it for about ten-seconds. It looked as if it was swimming, but flying in the air. What could this creature be?

I'm kind of freaked out by this. I jumped on the internet as soon as I got home and thank gosh, I'm not the only one." AR

I contacted the witness for further information. It seems the sighting was between the Casa Blanca Country Club and Lake Casa Blanca located in east Laredo, TX. The witness was driving north / northeast on Rt. 20.

JULY 1, 2013 – PALMDALE, CA

I RECEIVED the following account the next day after the sighting:

"My friend and I witnessed an unusual creature last night in Palmdale, CA that had us both confused and creeped out. It was around 3:30-4:00 am and we were hanging outside on my friends driveway. We saw this big bright white creature swoop from his neighbor's roof and with great speed flew in a tree and disappeared. It happened so fast we didn't get the chance to really get a good look for details. But from what we saw shocked us both. It caught our attention on how fast it shot into the tree and how bright white it looked. We both can swear that it didn't have wings like a bird.

I tried researching a bright white bird seen at night and the nearest possibility for what I saw was a flying ray-shaped cryptid. But the only doubt I have was its speed, which was so fast that it looked like a bullet shooting into the tree. I wish I could know what it was because I could honestly say it was abnormal. It seems like a creature that is out of this world. I'll never forget it. It's a mystery I hope one day can be solved."
Michelle

I called the witness for further detail. There wasn't much more to add, though she is very curious as to what this creature is.

EARLY FALL 2014 – RICHMOND, IN

I RECEIVED the following report on February 9, 2015:

"This is very hard for me to publicly write about. It was so, so strange and I have only told a few people because they just think you are crazy. When you tell them you 'saw a sting ray fly over the street from one bunch of trees to another.' I mean, we are in Indiana; nowhere near the ocean, for one thing. But even if we lived by the ocean, why would a sting ray fly into trees?

Anyway, this is what I saw on my way to work one early fall morning last year around 6:30 am. It was light enough to see that early morning, plus there are street lights up and down the way I drive to work. I am approaching a four-way stop and no cars around, so I go. I am looking downhill, following the street and seeing no cars. I glance up a bit and see this huge sting ray looking thing fly from one side of the street, out of a group of trees. It flies over the street into another group of tree tops on the other side. I was astonished! This is the only word I can think of to describe it. I never had much of a reason to use that word, but that sums it up! I was like OMG! Well, I immediately started praying to the Lord. It was so weird. I felt like I wanted to cry. I was kind of afraid, even though many emotions ran through me after the initial astonishment. I kept asking myself if I had really seen what I just saw, over and over all the way to work.

Well, for days I could not stop thinking about it. I told a couple of people and they didn't believe me. I started to look at pictures on the internet to see what I might compare it to and I come across this huge Manta Ray picture and underneath it states 'Devil Ray' Then I look up on the internet about demonic creatures and sting rays. I come up with a bunch of stuff about water spirits. That is what I really think it was. Our town has been known to give people the feeling of a demonic hold or something. Now I believe it. This town has all kinds of problems and if you look up these water spirits you can see what they bring. Anyway, that's what I saw and now I have found you have others that have seen the same thing. This makes me so happy that I am not crazy! Thank you for posting these sightings." TS

I contacted the witness and received more information:

"The location was in Richmond, IN between S. 16th & E Streets and S. 12th & E Streets overhead. I was driving west on E Street.

It was grayish (shark-like) on top and whiter on the bottom, but it looked just like a giant sting ray gliding over the street. We lived in Florida for years and there are a lot of petting places that have star fish, sharks, turtles and sting rays so I have seen these things up close. It is hard to explain but you know how the edges of a sting ray wave as it glides through water? Well, the edges of it were doing the same thing but through the air. I barely saw the long tail thing from the back as I was watching the edges of it wave and glide.

There is a river (East Fork of the Whitewater River) if you continue down E Street west you would run in to it. This would be S. 1st Street. I go over the bridge to my work." TS

The area of the sighting is a mix of residential & commercial properties on a two-lane road. The witness' description mirrored that of an actual Manta Ray, with very little deviation. It's unusual for one of these cryptids to be seen in populated location, but I truly feel the witness observed what she described.

NOVEMBER 2, 2015 – INGLESIDE, IL

I received the next account on November 20, 2015:

"I witnessed something I can't explain. Maybe you can help. It was Nov. 2nd about 6:30 am I was driving to work eastbound on E. Grand Ave in Ingleside, Illinois. I had just passed the Gavin Elementary School and saw what looked like a sting ray or manta ray flying across the road, not far from Fox Lake. I almost ran off the road. It must have been twenty feet long and about fifty feet over the road. It was a light gray color but not shiny like metal. It was a dull light gray. It reminded me of a smooth plastic tarp. It wasn't going very fast. There were a few cars coming in the opposite direction but they didn't react from what I could tell. I know it sounds weird but I swear that this is what I saw. There was no tail, but was shaped like a sting ray fish. There was no flapping of the wings. It just glided across the road towards the preserve and Long Lake. Can you help me out with this?" SH

I emailed the witness the same day and received some follow-up information:

"It was probably twenty feet long and twenty feet wide at the wings. There were no markings though there may have been some small structures underneath towards the middle. I could not distinguish what it may be. There was no sound from what

I could tell. It was traveling on a straight course, but I soon lost sight of it after it flew over the road. It may have dropped in altitude. There have been UFO sightings in the area in the past. We're not that far from Lake Michigan and north of Chicago. I appreciate the information you sent about the flying ray-shaped beings. If I hear or see anything else, I'll contact you." SH

If this was indeed a flying ray-shaped cryptid / craft, the description is very similar to others I have received in the past. This particular example is much larger than any other reported to me. 20' x 20' is quite large and I would have expected some chatter coming out of that area. Again, we don't know what these objects are. I've suspected that it's a bio-form craft; possibly a mechanical / biological hybrid of some type. I also believe that not all people can visually distinguish these objects, simply because these sightings are mostly during the daylight and other people in the vicinity don't seem to notice it's presence.

11

FLYING ANOMALIES

This chapter includes those flying cryptids that are more questionable and mysterious than the previously acknowledged entities.

JULY 2012 – REEDLEY, CA

I RECEIVED the following account on October 31, 2013:

"It was July of 2012 and I was at my sisters house in Reedley, CA (Fresno County, California - San Joaquin Valley). This is in a residential neighborhood. There is a river that is very close by which is right next to the cemetery. Everyone was inside getting ready for bed and I was in the backyard with my son. We were sitting having a conversation about life and looking up into the night sky. I have to admit that I'm the type of person that is always looking up in the sky to try and find UFOs. But this night I was just relaxing looking upward. My son was talking and then all of a sudden in my right peripheral vision I saw what I thought was a bird flying down towards

the both of us. It looked like it had its wings spread open like it was about to land. There is a big palm-like tree in the distance and in my mind I thought it was an owl. These thoughts were quick. I turned my head in the direction of the thing to get a better look at it.

What I saw was a translucent bird-like object. It was light in color. The translucence reminded me of a jellyfish. I stood up and yelled out, "What the heck is that!" We both stood up and my son yelled out, "Where, where?" I said right there and pointed to the thing. It was about thirty feet off of the ground. He finally caught a glimpse of it and just muttered in disbelief. I couldn't believe what I was seeing. After we stood up, the thing banked to its right. Then you could see it from its side. It looked like it was gliding.

The backyard we were in was fenced in all the way around. There are no alleys in the neighborhood so your neighbors are right over the fence. The thing glided around the perimeter of the fence and flew over the neighbors backyard. The neighbor was directly behind my sister's yard. The really weird thing is that during the sighting it looked like it was changing shapes as it went in the different directions. Like I said before, when I first saw it, it looked bird-like. Then when it turned it looked like an oval shape. As it went over the back neighbors yard it looked like something was hanging off its wings or sides. It was almost like ragged wings. The further it flew the more it looked like an oval shape. The whole time the color and translucence stayed the same. Honestly, after the whole thing happened I thought I saw what people describe as a witch. Like a ghost witch. This thing was definitely there. We saw something. The wing span must have been about ten to fifteen feet wide." - DS

This flying being may have been similar to the 'flying ray'

phenomenon. The translucent qualities fit, though the shape-shifting is a anomaly I've not read previously. Again, this was also near water (Kings River).

JULY 1997 – BREMERTON, WA

I RECEIVED the following account on February 5, 2015:

"Hi, I've been searching the internet for years for an explanation of what myself and husband saw back in July 1997 in Bremerton, Washington on a warm summer night about 10 pm. These things began to glide over the evergreen tree line into the moonlight which made them visible.

There were two of them. Very large (wing span of Cessna airplane) transparent flying creatures flying or swimming high in the sky near the Bremerton beach & over my in-laws house. The head was clearly similar to a prehistoric bird with a pterodactyl type beak & although the body/wings reminded us of a sting ray (no feathers). It had feet and a long prehistoric bird like tail. They seemed to glide in the air.

They glided about ten feet above our heads (colorless & transparent) like Wonder Woman's airplane. Hold a glass under water and examine how that looks. You can clearly see the shape but not much more. That is exactly how it looked in the moonlight. It took on the reflection of everything around it, like reflective glass when the light hits it just right.

They made no noise, just completely silent. One swooped down so low that if we had stood on his dad's truck we could have reached up and touched it as it flew overhead. It glided above us and seemed to almost run into the neighbors house, then veered and glided down the street. It then flew into the darkness. We heard no wing flapping. It was silent.

None of the family believed us. I wouldn't have believed my husband except I saw it with my own eyes. We didn't feel threatened by them and they didn't seem to be stalking us, but rather cruising by.

I hope one day this mystery is solved, but I did think maybe it's two dimensions colliding for a brief time? It seemed so prehistoric. I'm religious so I had also wondered if it could have been spiritual." KP

Even though the descriptions were similar to pterosaurs, it seemed to have the same qualities described in many of the flying ray sightings I've been investigating over the years. Some of these factors included body shape, transparency, stealth, silence and near water. The state of Washington has a history of cryptid bird sightings, notably smaller pterosaur-like creatures. Were these manifestations or flesh & blood creatures?

JULY 6, 2005 – SAN MARCOS, CA

THIS EYEWITNESS ACCOUNT was forwarded to me not long after the sighting:

"The encounter occurred on July 6, 2005, at about 11:30 pm. I had a long day in San Diego, then afterward going to the beach at Del Mar, CA for some surf fishing. I arrived at my home in San Marcos about 11:00 pm. After cleaning my fish and showering, I was very tired. I went out to my carport for a smoke and a look at the night sky. I looked north, thinking about a recent UFO sighting and wondering what it's all about. In the distance, at a couple hundred feet, I saw a faintly visible moving object that flitted from side to side. Whatever it was, it reflected light from the streetlights. Its side to side

movement was so fast, I couldn't tell if it was one object or two. The object then zipped directly over my neighbor's house across the street.

By this time, I was certain I'd never seen anything like it. It continued to move side to side, in a space of approximately fifty feet. It then stopped and I observed it more clearly.

It had big 'eyes' and wing-like appendages, and was probably two to three feet in width. It remained still and I could see wavering reflections from its 'wings' which were not beating like a bird's, but showed shimmering reflections from the streetlights. I felt the hair on my head rise all the way down my back to my ankles! It appeared to be looking at me. I felt threatened and said out loud, "I see you!" Then it went from stationary to out of sight, right over my head in an instant. I came out from under my covered carport, and turned to follow its movement. Immediately, it zipped into view directly above my head, obviously studying me! I could see weird large and intensely dark 'eyes.' It seemed surprised by my looking right at it. It didn't like being seen. My apprehension rose even higher. It turned away and disappeared like a shot.

It had a bird-like shape, but was thicker. It wasn't a bird, bat or any familiar nocturnal creature. Its movements did not seem explicable in comparison to any creature that flies by beating its wings. The hills and mountains are so rugged and inaccessible near my home, that anything could remain hidden and make night time forays at will." NN

MAY 5, 1985 – ILCHESTER, MD

The following incident took place near a location where I

was working at the time. It was reported to me and then I subsequently conducted an investigation:

I was thumbing through old investigation files when I came across notations I had made in regards to an unknown bird-like creature. The sightings were reported in 1985 and continued into 1987. It was an odd situation because I knew a few of the witnesses and I was also employed nearby at the time of the sightings. Cryptid investigation was new for me since my main focus was researching hauntings, but I had studied local Bigfoot encounters and wanted to expand my paranormal focus.

During the afternoon of May 5, 1985, I received a telephone call from Alfred M., the initial witness. He and two other men had seen a large bird-like creature perched in a hickory tree while driving south on Thistle Rd. toward River Rd. adjacent to the Patapsco State Park in southwest Baltimore County, Maryland. Alfred stopped the vehicle and watched the creature for several minutes. It eventually flew out of the tree and landed approximately fifty feet from the road where the witnesses were able to get a keen observation of the creature. Albert stated that it stood four to five feet high and was greenish-blue in color except for the head which was bright red. The wing span was enormous. He estimated it at fifteen feet or more tip-to-tip. The legs were thick and long with distinguishable talons. The eyes were also noticeable; slanted and large with a bright yellow hue. It also made 'clucking and cackle' sounds. After a minute or so, it unfurled its wings and took flight towards the east. Alfred said it reminded him of a hybrid 'dragon and peacock,' which he thought was crazy but he stuck with the description. At the time, I thought that the creature was either a large turkey buzzard or maybe a peacock someone may have had as a pet.

In fact, a peacock farm did exist in the area back in the 1950s according to people I had interviewed. I went to the location but found no evidence supporting the sighting.

Later that year, I had heard a rumor of a large bird being seen near the Hilton Area of the Patapsco State Park on Hilltop Rd. After several inquiries I was able to locate the witness, Darlene M., who confirmed the sighting. She and her daughter lived nearby and had been walking along Hilltop Rd. when they observed a huge bird flying towards them. Darlene stated that the creature got within twenty feet of them then suddenly changed direction and flew into the woods. She said that they were terrified. She was sure it was going to hit them.

She had gone to the library to see if she could find a picture of the creature. She found an old illustration of a Fung Hwang, or Chinese Phoenix and said it looked very similar to what they observed. She described the head was a vibrant red with fierce eyes. The wings were leathery and tipped with large green feathers. It flew by so quickly that she was unable to get a better description.

Once again I was stumped by the sighting. I talked to two ornithologists who basically thought I was delusional. I also contacted the state park service and asked if they had heard of any strange reports. Nothing. Though they were amused by the questions.

On the morning of April 29, 1986, several employees at the local paper mill observed a large bird standing in the loading area. According to the witnesses, this creature fit the description of a very large peacock, but there were some oddities. The head was red in color and it didn't have the long plumes. Other than those anomalies the overall description pointed towards a peacock. Could there be a breeding population in the state park?

In January 1987, a truck driver (Robert S.) was heading south on Thistle Rd. and was startled by a huge bird that flew across the road in front of his vehicle. I was able to interview him by telephone a few days later (he lived in Edison, NJ). His impression was that it 'looked like a dragon.' There was snow on the ground and the creature was silhouetted well enough to get a quick but detailed look. Robert stated that it was 'as long as his truck was wide' and 'was powerfully built.' He also confirmed it had a red colored head and greenish-blue body and wings.

At this point I had nothing more than anecdotal evidence. There was no natural explanation for the existence of this creature. Even today I have little to go on because I simply have not come across another cryptid that matches the description.

The final sighting, as far as I know, took place on June 30, 1987. The witness, David, was a Baltimore Gas and Electric employee who, along with his partner, was working along the power line that runs north to south through the state park. At a point north of Hilltop Rd. near the old mill village is an abandoned church graveyard. The former church was razed in the 1930s but the graveyard was left on its own. Thus, it was severely overgrown by the woods. (I do think that the graves have been relocated since). David observed a large bird-like creature that he described as a 'gryphon,' though he admits that he didn't get a very good look at it. He only noticed the creature after hearing a rustling sound which he thought was probably deer moving through the woods. He said the creature rose up from a rock, spread its wings and vanished. David admitted that the sight of this beast was a shock and that he did not want to go back to the location.

I really wish I had more to offer. I kept the notes and vowed to go back and investigate the encounters if more sightings were reported. Unfortunately I have not heard of other incidents. Lon

SUMMER 2005 – CHICORA, PA

I received this account a few years after the incident:

"Lon - I'm an avid reader of your site and thoroughly enjoy hearing other people's experiences. Thanks for doing what you do - it helps me understand this mysterious world.

Anyway, back in the summer of 2005, I had a very unusual sighting, yet it was almost something of a blessing to witness (especially having such high hopes for such an existence!). Myself and an entire group of people witnessed a fairy close up. Nobody knew what to say. It started with a phone call from a friend, inviting me and my girlfriend at the time out to his parents house in the country areas of Chicora, PA. We accompanied a gathering of about seven or eight of us in total. It was a casual evening, nothing crazy and no drugs to induce any hallucinations. We sat on his parent's back porch as the sun set behind the trees (it was a nice house set in a thick wooded area) and carried on conversation amongst friends. Night came and nothing much else changed.

This porch was more of a deck. It was roughly ten by fifteen feet, which was a nice spread for all of us to gather around a table on. To the far side of the deck (which was right across from where I was sitting), my friend's mom had a huge pile of pots and plants that rested against the railing of the deck and the house, all of which sat right under the spot light for the deck. So our area (the deck) was very clearly visible in the dark. At this point, it was probably around 10 pm considering that it was almost pitch black outside.

Suddenly, during one of those odd quiet moments in conversation, we heard a pot 'tink' sound as if it were lightly bumped. Being out in the woods in the dark, all of us turned to see what kind of animal was spying on us. To our surprise, as we all turned to look (and mind you I had a front row seat the whole time), we saw what looked like either an enormous moth (and I've seen big moths, this thing was more like a squirrel's size) or a rather large bat shoot straight up from the pile of pots. However, this thing obviously had wings that were wrapped around its body like a tortilla. But I immediately noticed something that blew my mind. It had a human head with extremely long pointed ears, almost as if they were to be disguised as antennas. However, there was no 'human' hair on this creature. It shot straight up from the pile of pots. But what happened next totally threw us all in a spin.

It reached its maximum 'launch' height, and hung suspended in mid-air for about half a second when suddenly its wings burst open into a full spread, right in front of the porch spot light. I could not believe what I was seeing. It was a perfect slender human female body with wings attached along the entire side of its body, from fingertips to toes and then some. 'Her' body was solid and silhouetted against the light, but her wings resembled the skin of an ear lobe, almost like a bat's wings. Being in front of the light, I could somewhat see through her wings and actually saw the veins that carried blood throughout her body. Her skin, I assume, was a pale green pigment. I say 'assume' because her entire body and wings were covered in what looked like tiny white hairs. But there was something magical about her hair because it carried a definite soft green glow around her entire entity. I drew pictures to try to describe how she at first appeared wrapped up in her wings, and then how she opened up to a full spread 'X' figure. She was a combination of human and butterfly, with a biological twist of bat.

Now, biologically, I'd say she had the body density and weight of a large squirrel. About one foot in height and body proportions that seemed identical to a human. The wings were so oddly beautiful in design the way they attached to her body and 'stretched' at full wing span (which she had to do by opening both her arms and legs to get this full effect).

Now here's the next part that just doesn't make sense. Like I said, when she first shot out of the pots, she hit a high point where she was suspended in mid-air for about half a second and then burst open in an instant to reveal her truly graceful form, which again she hung in mid-air for another half second, making an overall second or two of hang time. But after she showed herself in this full spread form, as heavy as she seemed to be (having the seemingly biological makeup that I observed), she defied gravity and 'fluttered' right over top of the table, over top of all of us (about four feet above the table), and off the deck and into the woods. From point A (the pots on the porch) to point B (the woods) she probably fluttered for about seven to ten seconds. It was dark outside so once she left the confines of the porch, she left the radius of light that we could see in from the spotlight on the porch. She was gone in an instant once she crossed that line.

All of us sat silent for about thirty-seconds, jaws wide open, until someone burst into, "Holy shits!" and the sort. We all fumbled for an explanation for about five to ten minutes before we all just decided to accept what we saw; a fairy. Not one of us thought it anything else. Like I said, it for one-second while wrapped up in its wings resembled a giant moth or bat, but I could see that human head and instantly knew it was a humanoid. And once she opened her body to reveal her true *form, there was no mistake. It was a real life fairy. Absolutely beautiful.*

About an hour later, my girlfriend and I left and headed home. The whole ride home we could not stop speaking of what we saw and how it altered our perception of reality and the unknown (or lost) magics of this world. Do not ever stop believing and never turn your head from nature. That is when you stop seeing." JF

SUMMER 2016 NEAR BALTIMORE, MD

I received the following account on January 26, 2019:

"I live in the greater Baltimore area of Maryland, in a suburb in the woods near an early colonial settlement. I have experienced multiple phenomena that I cannot explain. Things I can only describe as cryptids. I hope you find what you are looking for in my story.

Regarding a bat-like creature, what I saw did not look like a bat, but it was large and had wings. It was very late on a summer night in 2016 and I was 18 or so. I had just gotten into an argument with my girlfriend and was sitting on my porch smoking a cigarette. In front of my porch was my short driveway that led to the street. This is a newer neighborhood and fairly well lit. I saw what can only be described as the silhouette of a large winged creature. The wingspan was at least six feet wide if not more. But I saw no body. No torso, no wings in the true sense. It was almost like a shadow of a large crane's skeleton. I know that doesn't make sense but that is how it appeared to me. The wings were but a thin projection like the bones of a bird's wings. There was no skin flap like in bats or feathers like a bird. The rest of the body was similar, more like the suggestion of a body in this shadow form. The way it moved is was truly terrified me.

I am an avid outdoorsman. I have seen cranes, geese, swans, hawks literally hundreds of times during hikes and camping trips. I have never seen an animal move in this way. It glided with a grace, a timelessness even, that I don't think a physical animal could manage. I was horrified. I ran down my driveway (it had flown directly overhead towards the street) but I did not see it again. I called my girlfriend crying. I was absolutely terrified." Alex

MARCH 2010 – CENTRAL VALLEY, CA

I received this next report soon after the incident:

"I was in a friends backyard and he suddenly starts telling me that he had been mowing his lawn and caught something out the corner of his eye. He looked up to see what he immediately called a 'Flying Man.' He looked at it for four to five-seconds and yelled out to his brother to come quickly and see this thing. His brother ignored him.

He drew the object and captured its simplicity.

He ran over and dragged his brother to the spot. His brother could not see it and walked away. He watched for a few seconds and again went and dragged his brother to the spot at which time neither could see it. Viewed from its left side and below, it was a seven foot tall man in a copper colored fitted shell that was metallic looking reflective material. It was 1:30 pm in the afternoon, bright sunshine and mostly blue skies. The object was ascending at a thirty-five degree incline at walking speed. From its elevation he thought it might have left the ground thirty-seconds prior. He estimates it was eighty feet away at about thirty foot elevation (right over a telephone poll he used for distance) and he had a clear unimpeded view. The object had a forward tilt, ski jumper attitude and was climbing slowly and silently.

The shape was immediately recognizable as a man wrapped in an aerodynamic shell. The hooded head and shoulders were smoothed together, the chest was large three feet plus across. It tapered down to what was obviously feet pointing down. - MJ

SEPTEMBER 17, 2013 NEAR OTTAWA, ONTARIO, CANADA

My colleague Jamie Brian forwarded the following information to me soon after he received it from the witness:

"My introduction to this subject began on the morning of September 17, 2013, in a small Canadian town of Maitland along the St. Laurence River in Ontario. I had just gotten my young son ready for school and onto the bus as I proceeded to enjoy a morning coffee on my day off. I continued to do a little work around the house until I received a call from an old friend in Ottawa who wanted to meet for coffee. It had been a while since I'd kept in touch after moving from the city of

Ottawa to start a family business for my parents earlier that year. So I decided to take advantage of the open schedule before needing to be home for my son after school later that afternoon, and left to meet my old friend in Ottawa.

I lived right beside the highway onramp and was on my way rather quickly on that sunny yet windy fall day. As usual, I put some good music on and proceeded to enjoy the approximately 1 hour long scenic drive to Ottawa. I rather liked and travelled this route quite often. It was an uneventful trip which had passed rather quickly as I began to approach the Ottawa city limits at about 12:20 pm. At this point, in broad daylight without a cloud in the sky, I caught my eye up ahead in the distance on what at first came to mind as very large seagull due to its white and gray appearance up in the sky. I still remember thinking to myself at the time, "That's a big seagull!"

Something was amiss, and within a blink or two I noticed that the wings did not match my initial interpretations. This was further away and much larger than at first perceived. I then noticed what looked like outstretched arms connected to a human looking torso with a head and what I call 'legs' but which in fact more closely resembled a long serpent looking tail flowing behind this winged being at the time. I do realize how strange this may sound, but I assure you that it is unfortunately all too real. The following events still go through my head incalculable times per day ever since they transpired several years ago. It was still far ahead as I continued driving my vehicle towards it at about 120KM/Hr. I could make out more and more details as I swiftly approached, even at this distance I could clearly identify this as a winged humanoid with a very dark body color, (initially described as being like wet clay) and a massive set of swan-like wings. These wings were seemingly oversized for its body and moved very slowly in almost 180 degree rotation nearly touching its wing tips at the top and bottom of its graceful movements during flight. It was still fairly far ahead of me and appeared to be descending slowly along its path which now paralleled the highway. The brilliant white wings took on a light grey appearance as they became shadowed from the bright sun by their own movements at times during flight. This was likely why I initially misidentified him as a seagull which is typically gray and white in color and very common to the region.

At this point I was beyond certain that I was not mistaken in any way in my observations. My eyes and attention were completely diverted towards this incredible sight. I was at the time unaware but after already observing this being for about one minute, that shock had certainly now taken complete hold of me. I was looking at something that just couldn't be real or actually happening to me. When suddenly another vehicle in the lane to my right came nearly into my path as I was also distracted and veering close to his traffic lane, we seem to have both noticed the near collision at the same instant, corrected our steering's, made a half second, "do you see that?" type of eye to eye contact and both looked back up at it in the sky simultaneously at that point to what had obviously been his focus at the time as well. He was driving a late 90s Buick of burgundy color and appeared to be a mid 40s Middle Eastern looking man with short hair and medium build.

Heart jumping from the near high speed collision, I could still see the being up in the air ahead as I looked back towards him as the road began turning slightly to the left bringing this being into clearer and clearer view now to my right side. Slowly descending to a height where I could now see him looking over at myself and the other cars on the busy road that day as he flew adjacent to us for what felt like an eternity. The part that still sends chills down my spine was that this creature was clearly humanoid, but not like any human. His facial expression seemed highly intelligent, yet he portrayed a disdain and contemptuous demeanor as he looked over and down upon us with a confident air of supremacy. It was difficult to grasp or convey how truly intimidating this was, my only stunned reaction was of absolute fear and awe.

His face was just as dark gray as the rest of his body, and he possessed a very square jaw line with warrior-like predominant cheek bones. He also had predominant eye ridges which casted deep black shadows over portions of his face, including to his upper center lip due to the shadow from its nose under the sun. Besides the fact that this giant winged being descended from the sky, was the sheer size, dark color and bulky muscle mass of his body that truly made this creature so fearsome. I estimated its height to be about twelve to fifteen feet tall when compared to the surrounding trees. Its wing span was disproportionately large for its body size stretching approximately twenty-five to thirty feet across and I even remember questioning at the time how such long wings would be stored when the creature was walking and not in flight. It was the most beautiful yet terrifying thing I have ever seen. I cannot over stress this statement.

This being, now just above tree top level began to glide as opposed to when its wings were flapping in full flight at its previous greater altitude. The wings were snow white as they nearly glowed in the bright sun and reminded me of those of a hawk in general shape and the way that the outer feathers were spread and angled slightly upward at the tips during this stage low level of flight. I now had a very clear horizontal side view of this winged beings' outstretched body. His forward reaching upper arms were as thick as I am, and nothing compared to the barrel-like size of his chest and back muscles. It was truly a supremely powerful being that would strike true fear in the bravest of men.

Curiously, as opposed to when the being was first sighted about a minute and a half earlier, it now had two legs tucked back together as opposed to the longer tail looking appendage that I had first observed. His head was now turned to his left looking directly at me at this point and it truly unnerved me and still continues to do so to this day. Looking eye to eye with this giant flying humanoid was a moment only surpassed by the tremendous shock, anxiety and fear that it produced.

After it flew over a thin row of trees, this being began to shift its body to a vertical position as he flared his wings out even more to slow down, now just a few meters from the ground, directly to my right approaching an open field ahead of us. His attention now diverted to his landing, I could see his arms and legs somewhat awkwardly positioning themselves for a balance point as his wings acted like a giant sail in the powerful winds during his last wings outstretched airborne moments. He landed about 75 feet away from me, directly to my right in clear unobstructed view.

At this time I could also clearly see the inner feathers on his wings blowing feverishly in the strong wind, they were down-like and soft near his body, while the further to the outside of the wings I looked, the longer, stiffer and more defined the feathers became. I'd previously thought in mythological cartoon-like terms that these beings were supposed to magically ascend, defying gravity with the accompaniment of light and singing, but not the case here, where it was clearly observed being affected by, and had to follow the laws of nature from what I saw. It was as physically material and interrelating with its environment as a bird, human or any other living creature would be.

I was at this instant just passing ahead of this being,

moving my view of him from the right passenger side window to the rear, and again the being turned his head and looked right at me staring back at him as I now drove blindly just to get one last look at the being before the converging tree lines now in between us began to obscure my final view. All I can really remember was him ominously keeping eye contact with me for as long as was possible. To this day, I am unsure if he wanted me to stop, was maybe surprised that I could see him, or perhaps just wanted to make his presence known? Either way, I will never be able to forget that instant of time when I looked eye to eye and face to face, with can be described as nothing less than a Supreme Winged Being.

It had no facial hair, but wore some type of headdress grey in color resembling the shape of a modern air force flight cap. As well I noticed that he wore his hair in braided or dreaded looking pigtails coming out from under its cap on either side of its neck hanging behind the ears going to the back of its shoulders. I could see from around its neck that it wore some type of tight fitting robe matching its skin in color and being thin enough that I could see its muscles right through it. Upon its landing I could clearly see each of its legs, so it was probably a one piece kilt-like garment that I was able to notice on the bottom half of his attire. He did not appear friendly or welcoming and I will never forget the last seconds that I could see him and his ominous glare towards my direction that we shared through my back window. The witness sketch included here is of this last moment which I could see it between the trees before it was obscured from my view.

I turned my head forward, seeing that I was again partially out of my lane due to the colossal distraction, then made a slight steering correction and noticed an Exit '66 sign' ahead as a reference to later determine the exact location of the event. Not 10 seconds later, the Ottawa skyline became visible from around the continual slightly uphill rightward bend in the road. I knew then, that this being had landed as close to my nation's capital as is possible while maintaining some degree of cover. This being was not exactly hiding either, as it paralleled one of Canada's busiest highways for nearly two minutes from what I observed. Had he landed just a field or two over to the east, he would likely have gone completely unnoticed. I still wonder if he wanted to be seen, or if he simply didn't care that we could see him. This creature had a wise and princely, yet beast like air about it.

He possessed a very serious and sophisticated nature which appeared as focused and determined as one on a mission of great importance. Ottawa is a beautiful city, but I don't believe that it was there to take in the sights. I suspect that 'someone' in Ottawa that day knows a great deal more than I do about this entity and its reasons for being there.

What I observed was beyond belief, even to my own eyes as I looked upon it. I can remember being unable to calmly mentally process this occurrence, as it did not fit my understanding at the time in any conceivable way. I did not ever think about, let alone believe in 'Angels'. Accepting this was not easy as it negated all that I previously thought I knew. All I can remember about my brief meeting with my friend was that I was too shocked to say a thing about what had just occurred. I am certain that I must have appeared quite disturbed by something. All I wanted to do was get home, sit in private, and wrestle with making sense what had happened and what I was to do about it. The shock was in all honesty, nearly too much for me, pushing my personal limits to the edge of their capacity. This weight consumes me in enduring ways and has undoubtedly affected the course of my life since that afternoon.

I remember watching the local news that night and the

following day, hoping that something had been reported by another witness. I did consider coming forward at that time, but was trying to build a business in the small community and feared ridicule or negative impacts from coming forward. Besides, what do you even say to someone without appearing to have gone over the edge? Even I felt as though it was too unbelievable for anyone to believe me even if I did tell them. I shared what happened with my brother, parents, son and his mother over the following days as I could not hide the shocking effect or the excitement and wonder from the event. Besides these close family members, I primarily kept the encounter to myself for the following two years, but slowly expanded the amount of those knew of this event's occurrence to some additional friends and researchers in hopes of learning more about my experience.

Due to the stigma and rarity of these events they are not as easily received by others as say reports of flashing lights or disc shaped objects commonly seen in the sky these days. Again, I am not and was not religious, thus was not as in many cases predisposed to wanting to see anything like this at the time of the encounter. I did not really think about or believe in angels at all before the event, but can no longer deny their physical existence, only our human understandings of them.

My goal is to find the others driving on the busy highway that day that I know saw this being as well. (There were at least fifteen other cars in close proximity to myself during this encounter). It has taken me years to come forward with what I saw and I've still only shared it with a handful of trusted people until now. As well, Ottawa is a government, military and technological center with many professionals that despite seeing this may understandably prefer to keep their pensions and stay out of the mental health institutions by keeping it to themselves.

Before this event, I would honestly have found it very difficult to believe such a description from any another person, even if they were trusted and very close to me. Understanding this, I'm uncertain as how to best convey this event to you in a way that I would have been receptive to, if this is even possible to share fully in words without seeing this winged being for yourself. I swear on my family, to The Most High, that my description of and sighting of this giant winged being are true and as accurately described to you as is humanly possible. Thank you for listening to my experience, and again I do not share this in the interest of personal gain be it financial, egotistical or otherwise, but as something for the greater benefit of all.

My witness sketch is a close depiction of what was observed; except that the pencil that I used to shade the body does not exactly match the deepness of the grey body color actually witnessed which more closely resembled the color of

*the serpent pictured below. Pardon the condition of the
picture, as it's been a little soiled in its travels over the years,
having being hung in my bedroom and used as the cover to my
handwritten notes for some time."* EDS

After talking to the witness, he calls this being 'The Ottawa
Angel.' I know of a similar sighting in western New York, west
of Buffalo. That incident wasn't as detailed, but the size and
description is very similar.

12

THE SEARCH CONTINUES

This casebook is dedicated to those seeking the truth. I have been fortunate to be associated with researchers and investigators who have committed their personal time and effort to finding answers to these never ending mysteries.

So, let's take a brief step back in time and examine a few winged cryptid legends.

I received the following email from a man who lives west of San Antonio, Texas near Medina Lake. He states he witnessed a large flying creature on August 11, 2009:

> "Dear Sir, I witnessed a large flying creature this evening that I cannot identify. I found your site during a search. I'm apprehensive of mentioning it to any friends or family until I can get a grip on what this was.
>
> I live west of San Antonio, TX near Medina Lake. Today, I was on a random outing to the area near the Diversion Lake dam. At about 7:30 pm, I was on my way back up the trail when I suddenly heard a loud awful scream coming from below the dam downstream. It sounded like an owl but lasted

longer and was much louder. I stopped walking and watched downstream to see if I could catch a look at what caused the sound.

I then noticed a large flock of birds flush out of the trees near the riverbank. Then suddenly this giant flying creature swooped down into the river valley and just as quickly flew back up into the rocks. I continued to watch but did not hear or see it again. I call it a creature because it looked nothing like a bird. I was about fifty yards from it and would say conservatively that it's wing span was fifteen feet or so! It was dark colored and had a very long beak and a strange long thin tail. This sounds crazy, but it actually resembled one of those flying dinosaurs though the head was not as large and it looked like it had feathers.

I got back home and looked on the internet for examples of bird species but found nothing close. I'm not originally from this area and have never heard of anything like this. That is why I'm contacting you. Do you have an idea what it was? I see you have a website, maybe someone who reads your site could help identify it." JJ

I looked back at a 2007 interview between folklorist David Zander and cryptozoologist Ken Gerhard that mentioned the legend of the Thunderbird.

Myths and legends about creatures from the Chupacabra to the Jersey Devil to Bigfoot are everywhere, but in southern New Mexico and parts of Texas people say they've seen birds so big they seem prehistoric. David Zander claims the rugged landscape near Las Cruces hides a mystery that's haunted him for several years.

Zander has lived near the Doña Ana Mountains for more than forty years. Much of his time was spent hiking, exploring and fossil hunting in the range between the Robledo and Organ Mountains. He witnessed something that he's unable to explain; two creatures perched on a mountain less than a mile away.

"These creatures were so huge they looked like the size of small planes," Zander said. "All of the sudden one of them jumped off dropped off the top of the mountain, came down the front of the mountain and all the sudden these huge wings just spread out. I would say the wings were at least a twenty foot wingspan."

"Not a normal bird, definitely of a giant variety," Zander continued. "It makes you feel like it could come over and carry you off if it wanted to."

One ancient bird in the vicinity is an Andean condor. But its wingspan of twelve feet pales to what Zander described; birds with an unprecedented twenty-foot wingspan, with pink bald heads and all-black bodies, and feathers on their enormous wings. There is nothing on modern record like it.

"In comparison a twenty foot wingspan would truly be a monster and something undocumented by science," cryptozoologist Ken Gerhard said. "I believe what Dave Zander may have seen are surviving teratorns."

"What's interesting the reports of these giant raptor-like birds to continue into modern times," he said. "We seem to have a large concentration of them here in the Southwest particularly in the Rio Grande Valley of Texas as well as New Mexico and parts of Arizona."

Gerhard said his research falls into two different descriptions from witnesses. Some said the birds look like the prehistoric pterodactyl while others, like the creatures described by Zander, resemble the ancient thunderbird from Native American mythology.

You can find thunderbird images atop many totem poles and also carved into the lava rocks of the Petroglyph National Monument in Albuquerque. Similar images are found in petroglyphs all over North America.

According to legend, the thunderbird is said to have a wingspan the length of two canoes with the ability to deafen people with the sound of its flapping wings.

In March 2010, Jc Johnson of Crypto Four Corners contacted me about an incident where twenty-four sheep were mutilated at a farm near Hogback, New Mexico, on the Dine' Navajo Reservation. The livestock owner explains that there were large talon marks but very little blood and no evisceration. Was this an attack by a large flying predator? Why were the carcasses left intact?

Jc mentioned that a large cryptid bird or pterosaur may have been responsible for this act. That theory is not as far-fetched as it may initially sound. For many generations, people in New Mexico and parts of Texas say they've seen birds so big they seem prehistoric.

But these reports of large cryptid birds have not been confined to the American southwest.

My friend and colleague Butch Witkowski provided the following vintage Pennsylvania 'Thunderbird' sightings by non-native witnesses.

Once known as the 'Forbidden Land,' the Pennsylvania Black Forest region encompasses Clinton, Potter, Lycoming, Tioga, Cameron, and McKean counties. Predominantly sparsely populated state forest and game lands, it has been haunted for centuries by giant birds known as 'Thunderbirds.'

The earliest known account is that of Mrs. Elvira Ellis Coats, who claimed to have seen Thunderbirds in the 1840s McKean County.

In 1892, a farmer in Centerville caught a bird eating a dead cow at the edge of his field. Former Potter County School superintendent,

A. P. Akeley, saw the bird and said, "its color was gray. It stood upright. He is not sure how tall it was, but certainly over six feet and perhaps as much as eight feet."

Near Coudersport in 1940, a huge bird spotted "between six and eight feet tall... like a very large vulture. its wing spread was equal to the width of the road."

In August, 1945, the school bus left Helen Erway off by Ole Bull two miles from home because the dirt road had been oiled. After walking near a stretch of pines along the road she saw a large shadow on the ground. Overhead was a very large bird. She feared being carried off, so she ran until a neighbor stopped and drove her home. "It was not an eagle. The wings were straight out. It made a high pitch noise. The shadow on the road was about thirty feet." she said recalling the incident. Erway suffered severe nightmares and could not sleep or eat.

Finally her parents took her to her grandmother, Marion Erway, an Indian 'medicine woman,' who told her she saw a Thunder Bird. That it was there to protect her because she was part Indian. Her grandmother said it was a magic moment and that Helen shouldn't be frightened. Helen Erway also told of a 'thunderbird' hovering over Delbert Schoonover, when he was bitten by a rattlesnake by the dam, until help arrived. Other loggers who came to assist him also saw the bird.

Late one afternoon, Charlie Passell and others sighted a 'thunderbird' west of Renovo in late May 1964. The bird was spotted perched in a dead Hemlock tree at a strip mine near

Bush Dam. "Where the wing meets the body was thick, longer neck than a hawk's but not as long as a stork or crane, bigger beak than an eagle," he said. Passell heard of 'thunderbirds' and figured "that's what we must've seen because it wasn't like any bird we were familiar with. Definitely no eagle. Larger than a buzzard, real large."

The Egyptian tales of flying snakes captured the curiosity of the Greek historian Herodotus (ca 460 BC). These winged drakontes were said to live under frankincense (Boswellia) trees in the Arabian Desert. To gather the incense, the Arabians burned styrax (resin of the Liquidambar tree) because the smoke drove the winged snakes away. Herodotus described the flying reptiles as small with variegated markings, shaped like a water snake but with wing like membranes, like bat wings.

Flying serpents and snakes are also mentioned in 'The Hebrew Bible' and 'The Book of Mormon,' sent by God to control humans. 'The Book of Enoch' talks about the Watchers; supposed Angels dispatched to Earth to watch over the humans. They soon begin to lust for human women and, at the prodding of their leader Samyaza, defect en masse to illicitly instruct humanity and procreate among them. The offspring of these unions are the Nephilim, savage giants who pillage the earth and endanger humanity.

Eventually God allows a Great Flood to rid the earth of the Nephilim, but first sends Uriel to warn Noah so as not to eradicate the human race. The Watchers are bound "in the valleys of the Earth" until Judgment Day.

I could go on and on with description comparisons of venerable flying beings and those winged cryptids reported in recent times. But there is convincing anecdotal evidence that many of these legendary winged entities are connected to modern sightings.

I personally believe that many of these winged cryptids are corporeal beings that are able to manifest on our plane of existence. Their point of origin and means of conveyance is speculative. But this is the reason why we research and investigate this phenomenon. The search continues.

ABOUT THE AUTHOR

Lon Strickler is a Fortean researcher, author, and publisher of the syndicated 'Phantoms and Monsters' blog. He began the blog in 2005, which has steadily grown in popularity and is read daily by tens of thousands of paranormal enthusiasts, investigators and those seeking the truth. His research and reports have been featured on hundreds of online media sources. Several of these published reports have been presented on various television segments, including The History Channel's 'Ancient Aliens,' Syfy's 'Paranormal Witness', 'Fact or Faked: Paranormal Files,' and Destination America's 'Monsters and Mysteries in America.'

He has been interviewed on hundreds of radio & online broadcasts, including multiple guest appearances on 'Coast to Coast AM.' He was also featured on Destination America's 'Monsters and Mysteries in America' television show for 'The

Sykesville Monster' episode. Lon has written eight books and is currently the host of Arcane Radio on Beyond Explanation YouTube channel.

Lon was born and raised in south central Pennsylvania, near the Gettysburg National Military Park and Battlefield. After living in the Baltimore, MD metro area for forty years, he eventually moved back to his hometown in 2016.

ALSO BY LON STRICKLER

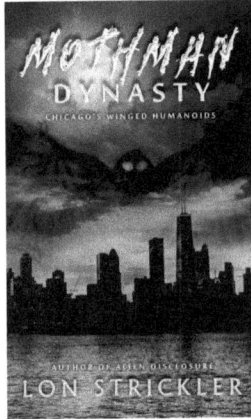

Mothman Dynasty: Chicago's Winged Humanoids

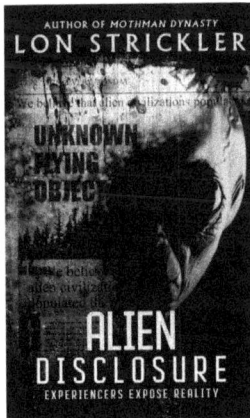

Alien Disclosure: Experiencers Expose Reality

www.ingramcontent.com/pod-product-compliance
Lightning Source LLC
Chambersburg PA
CBHW071018280326
41935CB00011B/1396